This is
CANNABIS

NICK BROWNLEE

CONTENTS

INTRODUCTION

'The music seemed to creep up through the heavy carpet, to ooze from the walls, to flurry, like snowflakes... It was just such music as a boatful of fairies sailing about in the clear water of the fountain might have made, or that with which an angel mother would sing its angel babe to sleep. It seemed to enter every fibre of the body, and satisfy a music hunger that had never before been satisfied. I silently filled my second pipe and was about to lapse again into a reverie that had become delightfully full of perfect rest and comfort when my companion, leaning toward me, said: "I see that you are fast approaching Hashishdom. Is there not a sense of perfect rest and strange, quiet happiness produced by it?"'

- From A Hashish-House In New York, HH Kane, 1883

'The sprawled body of a young girl lay crushed on the sidewalk after a plunge from the fifth storey of a Chicago apartment house. Everyone called it suicide, but actually it was murder. The killer was a narcotic known to America as marijuana and to history as hashish. It is a narcotic used in the form of rolled cigarettes, comparatively new to the United States and as dangerous as a coiled rattlesnake. How many murders, suicides, robberies, criminal assaults and deeds of maniacal insanity it causes each year, especially among the young, can only be conjectured... No one knows, when he places a marijuana cigarette to his lips, whether he will become a joyous reveller in musical heaven, a mad insensate, a calm philosopher, or a murderer.'

- From Marijuana, Assassin Of Youth, H Anslinger, 1937

The cannabis debate is very straightforward. You're either an establishment square who wants it outlawed as a menace to society, or a hippie deadbeat who wants it legalized in order to promote love and peace. Trouble is, the argument has never been as simple as that. Where once it was a highly useful source of fibre, food and medicine, at the beginning of the 21st-century perceptions and preconceptions about cannabis and its use have never been more blurred.

Leading police officers are prepared to turn a blind eye to users caught in possession but other equally high-ranking officers want it stamped out. Doctors and scientists spend millions investigating its medicinal value yet for every positive piece of research, there is a negative. Hundreds of thousands of tourists take weekend trips to Amsterdam in order to sit in cafés and smoke copious amounts of dope free from molestation, yet they risk prosecution for taking less than 30g (1oz) back through their own country's customs. And, after years of denial, top politicians admit to smoking cannabis in their youth, but, most bizarrely of all, an American President admits smoking a joint but not inhaling.

This book does not aim to preach the benefits or the deficits of cannabis. Instead, it aims to provide an authoritative guide to its history, laws and culture as they stand in the world in the new millennium, as well as its effects on health and the booming commercial business side of producing cannabis.

Over 4,700 years since its first recorded use, modern society's relationship with the cannabis sativa plant, and more importantly its active ingredient delta-9-tetrahydrocannabinol, has never been more complex.

In fact, it does your head in, man.

'Everybody smokes dope. The policy is just monstrous, completely out of touch with reality. Have I smoked it? Certainly, of course. Very seldom, now, but I would unhesitatingly have some – and why not? It's lovely. All young people do, too. How dare the Tories [British Conservative Party] interfere? Two-thirds of violent crimes are associated with alcohol. What percentage is involved with pot? Absolutely none. It doesn't make for violence; in fact, you become quite boring. It's outrageous that it isn't freely available.' – Lewis Wolpert, British biologist

If there is one thing that means more to pot-heads than the pot itself, it is the rich culture that surrounds cannabis and those who partake of it. Perhaps because of its ancient mystical and spiritual roots, because of the psychotherapeutic effects of the drug and because it is illegal, even the very act of smoking a joint has deep symbolism. Cannabis has evolved its own language, humour, etiquette, art, literature and music. Its culture is jealously guarded by those who are a part of it and derided, misunderstood – possibly even feared – by those who don't.

'One's condition on marijuana is always existential,' explains the novelist Norman Mailer. 'One can feel the importance of each moment and how it is changing one. One feels one's being, one becomes aware of the enormous apparatus of nothingness – the hum of a hi-fi set, the emptiness of a pointless interruption, one becomes aware of the war between each of us, how the nothingness in each of us seeks to attack the being of others, how our being in turn is attacked by the nothingness in others.'

To those who use cannabis, Mailer's description of the experience of smoking it probably makes eminent sense. To those that don't, it no doubt sounds like the typical esoteric ramblings of a dope fiend. 'Marijuana inflames the erotic impulses and leads to revolting sex crimes,' claimed the British paper the *Daily Mirror* in 1924, a verdict that still makes more sense than Norman Mailer to a great number of people around the world.

To others, it is not cannabis but the surrounding culture that is hard to take. 'I smoked cannabis a few times with my mates and it was okay,' recalls Colin Byrne, a 28-year-old teacher from Belfast, Ireland. 'But I couldn't get away with all the bollocks that went with it. All the etiquette, all the terminology, everything. It was like my mates, who were just yobs from the backstreets of Belfast, thought they were San Francisco hippies. "Pass the doobie, man," and "Hey, this is great shit." It was pathetic, really. I just wanted to give them a good shake and tell them to stop being a bunch of posers.'

Colin Byrne's experience is neatly summed up by the *New Columbia Encyclopaedia* when it suggests: 'Much of the prevailing public apprehension about marijuana may stem from the drug's effect of inducing introspection and bodily passivity, which are antipathetic to a culture that values aggressiveness, achievement and activity.'

The culture of cannabis is, essentially, the manifestation of this 'introspection and bodily passivity'. The clichéd image of a typical pot smoker is of a slacker who lies around all day listening to The Grateful Dead, gladly evading work and anything that might contribute to a useful existence. It is this image more than any other that has stoked the ire of generations of anti-cannabis campaigners. In America, in particular, the cannabis culture has been perceived as an anti-American culture – and, more to the point, the culture of blacks, Indians and Mexicans.

Yet this image is a relatively modern concept. Cannabis has been consumed in various forms for almost 5,000 years – and for most of that time it was prized as a pick-me-up. 'I began to gather the leaves of this plant and to eat them,' wrote the 13th-century Persian monk Heydar, 'and they have produced in me the gaiety that you witness.'

Even as recently as 1895, a correspondent from the *New York Herald* was breathlessly reporting that, 'During the full moon, the Nosairiyeh tribesmen of northern Syria hold a ceremony that involves the consumption of enormous amounts of hashish. The ceremony begins with the ritual sacrifice of a sheep, after which a large earthenware bowl filled with liquid honey-hash is passed around. A bundle of cannabis leaves are attached to the base of the bowl. After drinking this concoction, the eyes of the Nosairiyeh brighten, their pulse quickens, and a restlessness takes possession of their body as they start to dance.'

This account tallies almost exactly with the observations of the Greek historian Herodotus from 2,500 years earlier, when he came across Scythian tribesmen getting high on cannabis fumes: 'They make a booth by fixing in the ground three sticks inclined toward one another, and stretching around them woollen pelts, which they arrange so as to fit as close as possible: inside the booth a dish is placed upon the ground into which they put a number of red hot stones and then add some Hemp seed... Immediately it smokes and gives out such a vapour as no Grecian vapour bath can exceed; the Scyths, delighted, shout for joy.'

But it is the widely different modern cannabis culture that is most interesting, because it represents the extraordinary effect of this most ancient drug on societies that pride themselves on their pragmatism and sophistication.

ARE YOU GOING TO SAN FRANCISCO? – HASH AND THE HIPPIES

If there is one era that sums up the glory years of modern cannabis culture, it is the late 1960s in America. Freed from the austerity of the post-war years, and unwilling to subscribe to the Norman Rockwell idyll of their parents' generation, young Americans discovered a voice of their own through music, sex, travel and dissent – all of it borne along on a cloud of marijuana smoke.

In many ways, cannabis was the obvious accessory for rebellion. Throughout the 20th century, it had been vilified by the authorities as a substance that was the ruin of America's youth. Harry J Anslinger, the government official who was at the forefront of the anti-cannabis movement (see pp50-4), had been almost rabid in his attacks on the evil weed, engendering an irrational paranoia of the drug throughout the land. By the 1960s, however, Anslinger's propaganda had run its course and there was a new mood spreading through the USA. Young men were being drafted to fight in Vietnam and were returning in body bags. Those who survived returned to find that their country regarded them as failures. A new generation was growing up disowned, disillusioned and with no compunction to live up to the clean-living all-American ideal that had betrayed them.

More importantly, almost all the draft who went to Vietnam lived through the daily horrors they faced by smoking marijuana. Those who returned introduced it to other young people and its use quickly became widespread. By the late 1960s, a whole counter-culture had emerged whose desire was to drop out of society and the drug of choice was cannabis. The 'hippie' movement had begun.

In the US, the centre of cannabis culture was found in San Francisco. It was there, in the Longshoreman's Hall, that the psychedelic era kicked off in 1966 when a group of hippies staged what they called the Trips Festival. In nearby Golden Gate Park in 1967, an area of the park called the Polo Field played host to a massive outdoor concert/love-in called the Human Be-In. Special guests included Jefferson Airplane and beat poet Allen Ginsberg. In Haight Street, the epicentre of the hippie movement, and on adjacent Ashbury Street, the pot-smoking hordes hung out in head shops – specialist outlets selling hippie paraphernalia – lit incense candles, meditated and bartered for Hindu artwork. One of the main attractions was the Psychedelic Shop, which sold all sorts of hippie items – including dollar bills with Grateful Dead singer Jerry Garcia in the middle. The City Lights Bookstore, founded by Lawrence Ferlinghetti, boasted the cream of hippie intelligentsia. In its basement Allen Ginsberg first recited his poem, 'Howl' – this event supposedly kicked off the whole beat movement and it is chronicled in Jack Kerouac's seminal hippie novel *On The Road*. Fillmore Auditorium became the 'primal venue', where hippie guru Bill Graham hosted such top acts as The Doors and The Byrds.

Meanwhile characters like Ken Kesey were hitting the headlines with their distinctly unorthodox lifestyles. Kesey, author of *One Flew Over The Cuckoo's Nest*, was a former soldier who, in the early 1960s, was the subject of LSD experiments by the CIA. His mind scrambled by his experience,

Kesey dropped out of mainstream society, founded a gang called the Merry Pranksters and began touring America in a bus named 'Further', smoking dope and distributing LSD to the nation at a non-stop road party he called the 'acid test'.

The pinnacle of the hippie revolution in the USA, and in many people's opinion the ultimate example of cannabis culture at work, was the Woodstock festival of August 1969. The festival attracted more than 450,000 young people to a pasture in Sullivan County, 160km (100 miles) from Manhattan. For four days the site became a counter-cultural epicentre where drugs were consumed freely and sex was enjoyed virtually non-stop. The festival closed the New York State Thruway and created one of the nation's worst traffic jams. It also inspired a slew of local and state laws to ensure that nothing like it would ever happen again. The festival, which ultimately cost more than $2.4 million (£1.7 million), was sponsored by four wealthy young preppies called John Roberts, Joel Rosenman, Artie Kornfeld and Michael Lang. Roberts, the 26-year-old heir to a drugstore and toothpaste manufacturing fortune who also had a multi-million dollar trust fund in his name, supplied the money. He also had a University of Pennsylvania degree and a lieutenant's commission in the US Army but was fascinated by the hippie culture that was growing up among his generation. By early April, the promoters were carefully cultivating the Woodstock image in the underground press, in publications like the *Village Voice* and *Rolling Stone* magazine. The group settled on the concrete slogan of 'Three Days Of Peace And Music', calculating that 'peace' would link the popular anti-war sentiment to the rock concert and attract more punters. They also wanted to avoid any violence and figured that a slogan with 'peace' in it would help keep order. The big breakthrough came with the signing of the top psychedelic band of the day, Jefferson Airplane, for the incredible sum of $12,000 (£8,200) (the Airplane usually took gigs for $5,000 [£3,400] to $6,000 [£4,100]). Creedence Clearwater Revival signed for $11,500 (£7,800). The Who then agreed to play for $12,500 (£8,600). The rest of the acts started to fall in line. In all, $180,000 (£124,000) was spent on talent. 'I made a decision that we needed three major acts, and I told them I didn't care what it cost,' Lang said. 'If they had been asking $5,000 (£3,500), I'd say, "Pay 'em $10,000 (£7,000)." So we paid the deposits, signed the contracts, and that was it: instant credibility.' Woodstock was an enormous success and the defining cultural moment of the 1960s. It also sent a shudder down the spine of middle America, who saw pictures of young people off their heads and looking and behaving for all the world like savages.

But if the authorities regarded such activities with horror, they were powerless to stop them spreading. San Francisco and then Woodstock became a Mecca for young people from around the world, who were all too eager to return home with the good news. In Britain, cannabis made little impact on society until the 1960s. It was a country where alcohol was king, and where the only concern was stopping young people from drinking too much. If cannabis was used, it was usually by beatniks in London jazz clubs and by members of the West Indian community that had arrived in the country in the 1950s. But soon the authorities had a new problem on its hands. Influenced by bands like The Beatles and The Rolling Stones, who had become fully paid-up members of the hippie revolution, young people turned eagerly to cannabis. A full-page advert calling for the legalization of the drug was placed in *The Times*, the broadsheet of the establishment. Kids openly smoked dope in Hyde Park during a Rolling Stones concert.

> 43 per cent of British voters believed cannabis should be legalized completely for personal use. Among the 25–34 age group, the pro-cannabis lobby rose to 50 per cent.

'Everyone was trying it, but to be honest there wasn't a nationwide cannabis revolution,' recalls gallery owner John Lyons, 58, who was one of the thousands present at Hyde Park and who also took place in a pro-legalization march in 1969. 'To be honest I only remember the excitement lasting a few months. After that, it was mainly the die-hards who openly smoked it. I think the rest of us got bored with it.'

Nevertheless, the nation wrung its hands and only began to breathe easier when, in 1971, the government acted by reinforcing cannabis laws in the Misuse of Drugs Act. But by then, London and San Francisco were no longer the places to score and smoke dope if you were a true cannabis connoisseur. People were packing their kaftans and love beads and heading east, to where the karma was ambient and the dope plentiful and strong. So the Hippie Trail was born.

The Hippie Trail evolved out of Europe's beatnik scene, which was always very nomadic. For just a few notes, it had become possible to bunk down in cheap accommodation in ambient, cheap and dope-plentiful cities within Spain, Greece, Turkey and Morocco. By 1967 the scene had pushed beyond Istanbul to India, Nepal, and places further east. They called the journey 'the road to Katmandu'.

First stop was Tangiers, where boats and planes unloaded their cargo of wide-eyed pot-heads eager to follow in the footsteps of such earlier hashish explorers as Paul Bowles, Gertrude Stein and William Burroughs. From Morocco they headed to Istanbul – one of the major hash markets – then through the fertile plains of Iran and Afghanistan and finally to Nirvana in Goa and Katmandu. To a generation brought up in an atmosphere of repression, this was a whole new world just waiting to be explored. There were few laws governing the use and sale of hash. It was openly sold in coffee shops and bazaars. In Kathmandu alone, for example, there were more than 30 hash shops where the dope came in all sorts of shapes and colours.

Of all the venues on the Hippie Trail, however, Istanbul was the fulcrum, the last gateway to all points east for the thousands of wide-eyed hippies who thronged there in the 1960s. Here, for the first time, was the east in all its mystic glory: mosques, bazaars, horns, the non-stop hustle from hawkers and touts, and, of course, the pervading stench of the cheap, plentiful and indigenous hash. And, best of all, the laws were relaxed to the point of non-existence compared to the draconian anti-drugs legislation of Europe and the USA. While it was not advisable to be caught smuggling, and it was officially illegal to be caught in possession of dope, there was an abundance of illicit back-room smoking dens where it was possible to get stoned in peace.

Istanbul was also incredibly cheap. One of the most popular venues for young hippies to stay was 'the Tent', which was a corrugated iron and canvas shelter on the roof of the Gulhane Hotel in the centre of town. There, it was possible to pack down for next to nothing on the comfortable straw floor and indulge in all manner of social smoking with the other 'guests' who had washed up on the tide of western visitors. The dope was cheap too – thick slabs of Turkish hash for the same price as they would have paid for a miserly 5g (⅙oz) in the west.

Cities like Istanbul were also important news centres for travellers on the Hippie Trail – particularly when it came to exchanging information about where *not* to go. One no-go area was the Afghan-Iranian border. During the Shah's reign, if a traveller was caught with over a kilo (2¼lb) of hash, they would be tried by the Iranian Army Council and then shot. There were also stories about unfortunates apprehended in Tashkent doing hard labour in Soviet prison camps, or people who ended up being sent to Greek or Bulgarian prisons and were never seen again.

Yet, for all its dangers, the Hippie Trail was immensely popular. But it was incredibly short-lived. Ironically, it was the very availability of hashish that would spell the end for the Hippie Trail.

Increased demand led to inflated prices and large-scale smuggling, particularly from Nepal into India and abroad. Estimates in the mid-1970s claimed that more hashish was exported than consumed in Nepal. Inevitably, pressure on the Nepalese government to act soon came from the United Nations and the United States and, in 1972, they began to systematically shut down the hash houses. A year later, all hashish dealers' licences were revoked and the last of the hash hops were closed. The Hippie Trail had fizzled out for good – and with it the free and easy cannabis culture of the 1960s.

I DIDN'T INHALE – THE 1960s GENERATION GETS COY

Surprisingly for a generation who pushed back the boundaries of cannabis consumption, many children of the 1960s are today reticent about admitting they ever smoked – or indeed inhaled. This is especially true of those 1960s kids who went on to become political figures, especially those in the current UK debate about legalization. Jack Straw, the former Home Secretary, was a longhaired radical at Leeds University but claims to have never touched the stuff. The same is true of his successor in the Home Office, David Blunkett. Of the current batch of British MPs, only former Cabinet member Mo Mowlam has ever admitted smoking. Even the Labour MPs Claire Short, Tony Banks, and Paul Flynn, who have campaigned that the legalization of cannabis should be examined, flatly deny they have ever smoked marijuana themselves. Former US President Clinton famously admitted smoking a joint but not inhaling. And George W Bush, Clinton's successor, has denied using cocaine in the past 25 years but refuses to say anything about the years before that – suggesting that he too may have smoked marijuana but not inhaled... When pushed on the subject he admitted that he had 'made mistakes in the past' but would not engage in the 'politics of personal destruction' by talking further about the issue.

It has been left to old lags like Sir Paul McCartney and Sir Richard Branson to keep the 1960s flag flying. 'I think a liberal attitude is not a bad thing,' McCartney said. 'So I favour a decriminalization of it. If my kids ever ask me, "What about it?" I would say, "There is this bunch of drugs. This is probably the least harmful. There is a hit list. You can go up it to heroin but it's not easy, in fact impossible for some people". But I always say to them, "That's the facts of life, but if you ask my advice, don't do any."'

Richard Branson, the founder of British-based company Virgin, who signed a recent petition calling for the legalization of cannabis, said he would be prepared to sell the drug in his stores if it was legalized. He said his company would not want to get involved in selling ordinary cigarettes but he would not rule out promoting cannabis if the law allowed it because it is probably less harmful than tobacco. The millionaire businessman said that to encourage young people to smoke would be immoral. But although he was not advocating the sale of cannabis if it was legalized, he added: 'If a cigarette company started selling it at too high a price, I'm sure we'd be in there.'

CANNABIS AND RELIGION

Marijuana is closely connected with the history and development of some of the oldest nations on Earth. It has played a significant role in the religions and cultures of Africa, the Middle East, India and China.

Canapus   hanff   Caṗ·℈c·

Anapus latine·grece Canaps·arabice vero sechedenchi·
Serapio in dem büch aggregatozis in dem capitel Seche/
denchi id est canapus spricht daʒ diß krut werde gesetʒet vnd
brenget samen vnd hait eyn langen still vnd lange este vnd eynen
starcken geroch· vñ der stam ist inwendig hoel·¶ Paulus Canapus
ist ħ yß vnd drucken an dem andern grade· Welcher vilfeuchtikeyt

Illustration of the Indian hemp plane (*Cannabis sativa*) from a woodcut in *Gart der Gesunheit*, 1485.

Engraving of a male cannabis plant in flower, 1748. *Cannabis sativa* is native to northern India, where narcotic varieties are known as *bhang*. The drug is produced by resin glands on the surface of the plant as a defence against predators and is most concentrated in the flowering tips of unfertilized female plants. The male flowers, shown in this picture, are much less potent.

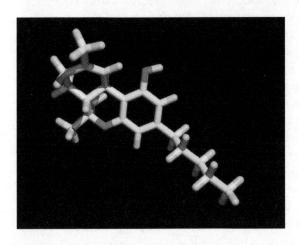

Molecular graphic of the active ingredient of cannabis, THC (tetrahydrocannabinol), with the atoms shown as sticks.

The shamanistic traditions of Asia and the Near East have as one of their most important elements the attempt to find God; getting stoned on cannabis has helped worshippers on their way. And in the days before joints, the quickest and easiest way to inhale the smoke was through cannabis incense.

In the temples of the ancient world, the main sacrifice was the inhalation of incense. In the Judaic world, the vapours from burnt spices and aromatic gums were considered part of the pleasurable act of worship. Stone altars have been unearthed in Babylon and Palestine, which were used for burning incense made of aromatic wood and spices – in many or most cases, a psychoactive drug was being inhaled. In the islands of the Mediterranean 2,500 years ago and in Africa hundreds of years ago, for example, marijuana leaves and flowers were often thrown upon bonfires and the smoke inhaled.

Today, cannabis continues to be the mainstay of the Rastafarian religion, which is discussed in detail later (see pp66–70). But the Rastafarians are not alone. One of the most controversial cannabis-based religions in recent years has been the Ethiopian Zion Coptic Church, a religion run by white Americans who claim its roots are in black Jamaica. The Coptics insist that marijuana, which they call by its Jamaican name, ganja, is their sacrament; as valid and as necessary to them as wine is to Catholics during communion. To many, including law enforcement officials, they are frauds – a group of rich dope heads who have been allowed to laugh at the law and get away with it.

Coptic services take place three times a day, but the Coptics partake of cannabis all day. One of their main centres is in Miami, where in the late 1970s they hit the headlines when they bought a house for $270,000 (£185,000), paid for in cash, which they promptly turned into a luxury commune with about 40 members. Trouble soon brewed when it emerged that Coptic women, and even the Coptic children, were encouraged to smoke marijuana. While it was the constant chanting and the smell of marijuana that upset close neighbours, it was scenes of Coptic children smoking marijuana on local television that brought protests from the city as a whole. Then, in November 1978, news broke of the mass deaths of the People's Temple cult in Jonestown, Guyana, and many Miami residents were shocked into wondering if they might not have a potential Jonestown on their doorstep.

In 1979, CBS news reporter Dan Rather interviewed one of their leaders, a former Catholic from Boston named Thomas Reilly, who preferred to be known as Brother Louv. Rather asked Brother Louv why the Coptics believed cannabis was sacred to their religion:

BROTHER LOUV: Well, let's start from the beginning, page one of the Bible, Genesis, Book 1, Verse 29: 'Behold, I have given you every herb bearing seed, which is upon the face of all the Earth...' Now, is there any dispute that marijuana is a green herb bearing seed that grows all over the Earth?

RATHER: All right, let's...let's address ourselves to the truth. Is the basic message, 'You should smoke ganja?'

BROTHER LOUV: The basic message is, 'You should stop your sin.' When you and I are neighbours and I have the security that you are a man who keeps the commandments of God, then I know you're not going to rob me, you're not going to murder me, you're not going to covet me. So that's the only security that people can have is to stop their sinful ways, stop becoming homosexuals when they know what the Scripture says about homosexuality; they know what wisdom shows you about destroying your own seed of life. They should stop their abortion. They should stop their birth control. They should stop their oral sex, their hand sex, and any way that they're destroying their own life and their own seed life. They should stop those things immediately. And they should have known to be smoking ganja from a long time. For how is it that I know to?

FROM BONGS TO HOT KNIVES – CANNABIS PARAPHERNALIA
To the casual observer, dope heads appear to spend most of their time on another planet. And indeed most do. But there is more than one way to skin up a joint – and when we consider the various methods of intake that cannabis users have invented, we can only applaud their ingenuity.

Also known as water pipes, *bongs* are designed to pass the smoke through water in order to cool and filter it. Grass is put in a bowl on the end of a tube, which has its other end in a sealed container partially filled with water. The tube at the end of the bowl is below the level of the water so that as smoke exits the pipe it is bubbled through a layer of water. The air pressure in the chamber is lowered by breathing through another tube that stays above the water level in the chamber. The advantages of the bong method are that the smoke is cooled and carcinogens are removed without affecting the active ingredients. Any liquid can be used to filter the smoke, although beer and other booze is not recommended as marijuana's active ingredients are soluble in alcohol.

A rather ostentatious method of smoking, these *pipes* are usually made of such heat resistant materials as stone, ivory, metal and glass and are often highly ornate. Grass is inserted in the bowl of the pipe and then lit. An alternative is the *stash pipe*, a pipe in which a small amount of grass can actually be stored. Some stash pipes are constructed in such a way that the smoke passes through the stash area so the grass inside is bathed in smoke and becomes coated in resin, making it a more potent smoke.

Glass hash pipes are used predominantly for smoking hashish or hashish oil. The material is placed in the bowl like it is with the other pipes, but instead of heat being applied to the top, it is applied to the bottom. *Gas pipes*, meanwhile, consist of an open-ended tube with a small bowl mounted near one end, perpendicular to the main axis of the tube. The end near the bowl is covered with the user's hand and the smoke drawn into the tube. When the hand is removed, smoke rushes into the lungs. *Tilt pipes* are for the connoisseur. These pipes have a heating element built into the pipe at the bowl. The element heats the marijuana to sub-flammable temperatures sufficient to activate and release cannabinoids from the plant material. The pipe is tilted to bring the grass in contact with the heating element.

For those who prefer to smoke on the hoof, *one hits*, also known as Dug-Outs, are small metal tubes with a cavity at one end and a mouthpiece at the other. The cavity is pressed in a container of grass until it is filled, then it is lit like a cigarette and inhaled steadily until all the grass is gone.

Hot knives are hardly complex, but powerful and efficient. Two wooden-handled knives are heated until glowing red. Small amounts of grass are then burned between the two knives while the smoker sucks up the smoke through a plastic bottle that has had its bottom cut off.

Cannabis can, of course, be cooked and eaten in a brownie. In Amsterdam coffee bars, 'space cake' is available for punters to nibble in between, or in preference to, smoking joints. For the uninitiated, it can often be easy to underestimate the power of these dope-laden snacks. 'I was in Amsterdam with some lads on a stag do, and we ended up in a dope bar,' recalls accountant Gary Miller, 32, of Nottingham, England. 'One of the guys was feeling a bit peckish so he decided to have some chocolate cake. He thought that even if there was cannabis in the mixture it wouldn't be strong enough to have much effect. The silly sod wolfed down about five of these cakes in two minutes flat. Within ten minutes he was absolutely stoned out of his brain and we had to take him back to the hotel.'

Perhaps the most famous 'space cake' recipe is the one dreamed up in 1954 by Alice B Toklas, lover of the writer Gertrude Stein and author of a cult cookbook. In it, she recommends taking 'one teaspoon black peppercorns, one whole nutmeg, four average sticks of cinnamon, one teaspoon of coriander. These should all be pulverized in a mortar. About a handful each of stoned dates, dried figs, shelled almonds, and peanuts: chop these and mix them together. A bunch of cannabis sativa can be pulverized. This along with the spices should be dusted over the mixed fruit and nuts and kneaded together. About a cup of sugar should be dissolved in a big pat of butter. The mixture is then rolled into a cake and cut into balls about the size of a walnut. It should be eaten with care: two pieces are quite sufficient.'

There are also a number of ways to get stoned by drinking cannabis. The easiest is to extract the active ingredients from the grass in alcohol and then use the tincture to make a potent drink. The highest-proof alcohol needs to be used – preferably 190-proof grain alcohol – since the water in alcohol will dissolve other chemicals in the marijuana. Another method is to heat the alcohol to sub-boiling point, then stir in the marijuana. The resulting emerald tincture is called Green Dragon and can be drunk straight, although this is not recommended. A cocktail is usually used, which consists of three parts lemon-lime soda, one part Green Dragon and a dollop of honey served over ice.

HASHISH HAVEN – AMSTERDAM'S CANNABIS CAFES.

The Euro 2000 football tournament, which was staged in Belgium and the Netherlands, saw the largest ever co-ordinated international police operation to crack down on the threat of hooliganism. It was understandable. The England team had qualified and, while it might not have hit the dizzy heights of success on the pitch since the World Cup of 1966, its so-called fans had ensured that, in the international hooligan stakes, the country was a world-beater. Not that England's yobs were about to have a pushover. For months, the Low Countries had been targeted as a potential battlefield where simmering rivalries between the leading hooligans of Europe – predominantly the English, Germans and Dutch – could resolve themselves in a fortnight of running battles to see who would be crowned top rottweiler.

But while the police girded their loins and polished up their batons in readiness for the invasion, the owners and sellers of some of Amsterdam's 300-plus cannabis cafés were putting forward their own unique crowd control strategy. Threatened with closure by the Dutch authorities for the duration of the tournament, representatives from the cannabis cafés began earnest negotiations with the Netherlands justice department, local police officials, and the local authority responsible for regulating the coffee shops and issuing licences for the selling and smoking of cannabis.

So it was that the cannabis cafés were granted late licences until after 1am, while others were allowed to erect giant screens so that fans from all nations could watch their team in action while getting pleasantly stoned.

'Fortunately, we made them see sense,' said a jubilant Roland Dam, the founder of Amsterdam's Cannabis College, which provides information on the industrial, medical and recreational uses of the weed. 'There is always less trouble when cannabis is involved. I mean, have you ever heard of anybody smoking a joint and then starting a riot? We are not saying that fans should come and smoke, but we are saying that smoking a joint is likely to contribute towards a more peaceful tournament. People will be very relaxed, they will be more objective about the games and they will also become a bit more tolerant if their team loses.'

Around 2,500 Americans pay for a round trip including fares, accommodation, and admission to attend the annual 'Cannabis Cup'. Billed as 'a week of sublime indulgence', they will sample, and vote on, the produce offered by a number of Amsterdam coffee shops.

In the event, despite minor scuffles in cities where England and Germany were based, the tournament passed off relatively peacefully. In Amsterdam, notably, there were no riots – even though the Dutch were knocked out of the tournament at an early stage.

For the under-the-cosh cannabis smoker in the UK and other countries, the cannabis cafés of Holland are a haven of which they can, as yet, only dream about having in their own country. And as a tax revenue for the Dutch government, there is no doubt that coffee shops make for excellent business. Sales of dope are estimated at around £500 million ($725 million) every year, of which the government takes its substantial share.

At most Amsterdam coffee shops, cannabis is sold either behind the bar or at a separate window. Most shops have a written menu and will show samples that can be bought in 1g or 2.5g bags or by the gram up to the new 5g (⅙oz) limit. Punters are also encouraged to blend different types of hash. A gram costs around £6 ($8.70).

True to the spirit of customer service, most outlets provide free rolling papers and little strips of cardboard for roaches. A few provide pipes and bongs for the more adventurous toker (deposit required). Dope bought elsewhere can also be smoked. However, coffee shops are not euphemistically named – it is considered extremely bad form not to buy something to eat or drink while you smoke. In Amsterdam's tourist district around Dam Square, some shops require that you purchase something before you sit down and get stoned.

Space cake, that cannabis-laced delicacy served in coffee shops, should be taken with caution, though. To the untrained, it can be mind-blowingly potent. Indeed, Dutch police have now got so sick of wide-eyed tourists wandering the streets in a caked-out paranoia that they tend to view edible cannabis as a hard drug.

Amsterdam has hundreds of coffee shops, and a glance at a typical menu shows that there is more to cannabis than an eighth of Black Leb. Varieties of cannabis include such exotic examples as Soma Skunk, Himalaya Gold, Diamond Shiva, and Reclining Buddha. Café owners are convinced that their existence exemplifies the benefits of cannabis within a civilized society. 'The message is, Don't do drugs,' says Ernst Gunst, owner of the Paradox Coffee Shop in Amsterdam. 'But if you want to use drugs, do it in a healthy, conscious way. One thing is for sure: if you forbid it, people still want to use it, like the US during Prohibition.'

Gerald Smiy, owner of Creamers Coffee Shop, believes he is offering a public service. 'Customers come in and ask for some hash or grass and I sit them down and talk to them about their choice. I ask them if they have smoked any before and if they say "No" I would usually start them off on some not-very-strong stuff to see how they go. If they say "Yes" I ask what they usually smoke and try to find something of about the same strength. I would also give them a leaflet telling them about how to use cannabis sensibly.'

Founded in 1975 the Bulldog is generally regarded as the oldest cannabis café in Amsterdam. It is also a prime example of how a laid back drug culture now marches hand-in-hand with shrewd marketing. Today there are now three Bulldog outlets in Amsterdam, including one on the main entertainment plaza, the Leidseplein. There is also a Bulldog cocktail bar, a Bulldog bicycle rental service and a Bulldog souvenir shop that sells T-shirts, denim jackets, caps, ashtrays, lighters, and rolling papers that all feature the Bulldog logo of a cartoon bulldog with a studded collar.

'The Bulldog is a social service and a whole philosophy,' says owner Henk De Vries. 'There is never a fight in the Bulldog. The customers and staff are too decent and sweet for that. By smoking hash or grass you get friendly, not aggressive.'

George Talbot, from Glasgow, Scotland, is a regular visitor to the city. 'It's magic, Amsterdam. Imagine if you lived here. You could smoke with whoever you liked – with your boss after work, after lunch on Christmas Day. It would be just like having a pint. And all completely legal. Maybe I'll move over here, get a job in a bar.'

But all may not be sweetness and light in the cannabis cafés of Amsterdam. Indeed there are some who believe they should be closed down for good. A leaked Dutch government report in 2002 suggested that the country's tolerance of soft drugs is creating a backlash of widespread illegal sales by criminal gangs who lure children into their net.

The report claimed that since 1999 the number of illegal outlets for drugs in towns with a population of fewer than 100,000 has risen sharply, but this is partly a consequence of the government's attempt to control the drugs scene by shutting down coffee shops. While the number of coffee shops has fallen from 1,200 to 840 in the past five years, the illegal drugs trade has expanded – including a substantial rise in the use of soft and recreational drugs among secondary school children.

Wim Van de Camp of the centre-right Christian Democrats party said: 'The current policy is not working. Coffee shops are not the answer and simply reducing the number of them solves nothing. It would be better to close them all down. Holland is the leader for drugs consumption and distribution throughout Europe. Unofficial estimates set the annual value of soft drugs exported from Holland at around 19 billion guilders [£5.5 billion/$8 billion].'

WE ARE THE CHAMPIONS – THE CANNABIS CUP

In 1988 the editors of American dope culture bible *High Times* had a brainwave: an annual jamboree of pot culminating in a competition to find the best marijuana and hash. Thus the Cannabis Cup was born, and as the world's premier showcase for pot there was only one place it could be held: Amsterdam.

Every year more than 1,500 people, ranging from inquisitive amateurs to expert aficionados, make the week-long pilgrimage to the coffee bars of Amsterdam in order to sample the variety of wares on offer. Celebrity judges are asked to present awards including Best Coffee Shop, Best Homegrown Pot, and Best Imported Hash.

Since its inception, the Cannabis Cup has developed into the dope equivalent of a sales convention. Bemused dope heads often find themselves harassed by company reps flogging drug paraphernalia from bongs to vaporizer units. In 1997 the first Hall of Fame award was set up and presented posthumously to Bob Marley. His widow, Rita, flew in from Jamaica to collect the award on his behalf.

In theory, anyone who attends the Cannabis Cup is allowed to be a judge. All that is required is some money and the ability to fill in the relevant forms. However, the main awards are presented by experts who really know their weed. And in order to remain truly objective, the judges sample each exhibit without smoking it. In order to do this, they have to know what they are looking for in each plant.

- Through a magnifying glass, they look for a thick coating of crystals and stalked glands topped with balls of resin. The weed should not be musty or dry and dusty when broken and rolled.
- A joint that is made with good cannabis should burn without constant relighting.
- A piece of hash that is sucked should have a peppery taste.
- By pressing a small amount in a hand they can tell quality as the quicker it darkens and softens the better it is.
- They will also burn a piece, look at it and smell it. The rate at which it burns is determined by the ratio of resin to plant matter. If it is fluffy, spongy or gritty and burns with brown-black, foul-smelling smoke, then the hash is predominantly plant matter. Denser, purer hash burns slowly and completely and gives off a pale-blue smoke with a pungent, spicy aroma.

CANNABIS CAFES UK STYLE

For British cannabis enthusiasts setting up their own Amsterdam-style cafés seems a logical step – especially as the laws are a great deal more lax than they used to be. But, as a number of hopeful marijuana entrepreneurs have discovered, the law still exists, and there are still police officers happy to apply it to the letter.

In 2001, James Ward from Manchester attended a training course in Amsterdam on how to run a cannabis coffee shop. He returned to England and, with an army of helpers, began to set up his own coffee shop in the south coast town of Bournemouth. Barely had the doors opened, than 60 members of Dorset police, plus a sniffer dog and its handler, busted the shop. Seven people were arrested for drug-related offences and a quantity of cannabis was recovered.

'Dorset police targets dealers and users in the more harmful Class A drugs like heroin and crack cocaine,' said Detective Chief Inspector Colin Stanger. 'But clearly we will not tolerate the dealing in and use of cannabis because it is an offence and our duty is to enforce the law.' At the same time, police in Rhyl, North Wales and Dundee in Scotland were warning potential café owners that they would not tolerate premises being opened on their patch.

Britain's first cannabis café, the Dutch Experience, opened in Stockport, Cheshire in 2001. It was raided by police on its first day, but supporters immediately reopened it. In the space of seven months, it was raided four times but remained open every day. On one occasion, cannabis campaigners – including two MEPs – marched on Stockport police station carrying cannabis, and demanded to be arrested. After 28 arrests, the police gave up, ignored anyone else possessing the drug and campaigners declared that it had in effect been legalized. The Dutch Experience continues to attract hundreds of people from across the country every day, but in December 2001 its co-founder Colin Davis was remanded in Strangeways Prison for breaking bail conditions on drugs charges.

More than a dozen other cannabis cafés are now being planned for Brighton, Liverpool, London, Edinburgh and elsewhere. They will certainly be raided by police and closed down – but all will inevitably open up again just as quickly.

GOTCHA – CELEBRITY CANNABIS BUSTS

The cannabis-crazy 1960s ushered in a new perspective on the weed. Prohibition was, for the first time, being questioned and the authorities were utterly bamboozled by the sudden and massive upsurge in recreational pot smoking. Anxious to show that they were in control of the situation, narcotics squads around the world sought out high-profile users to prosecute. And the celebrity world did not let them down.

In 1966, English folk singer Donovan was fined £250 ($360) for possession. 'I would like you to bear in mind that you have a great influence on young people,' the magistrate reminded him, 'and it behoves you to behave yourself.' But rock and rollers were far too busy getting stoned to allow such a weight of responsibility to affect their lifestyles. Rolling Stones Mick Jagger and Keith Richards caused a storm when police raided Richards' home in 1967. The police claimed both were high on pot, which they denied. Even so, they were sentenced to one year in prison and a £750 ($1,100) fine. The case went to appeal on the back of a public outcry over the severity of the sentence and was overturned on a technicality – the police hadn't found any pot on the premises. 'Pop stars should be subjected to a system of tests – like horses and greyhounds – before they go on stage,' wrote one affronted member of the public to the *News Of The World* in 1968. In 1976 pop pals David Bowie and Iggy Pop were busted in New York with an alleged 250g (9oz) of marijuana. They were later cleared. Ex-Beatle Paul McCartney famously spent ten days in a Tokyo jail after attempting to import 250g (9oz) of marijuana. He was later deported. In March 2000, singer Whitney Houston was allegedly found with 15g (½oz) of marijuana in her luggage at an airport in Hawaii. Officials later decided not to file charges.

Hollywood has also had its run-ins with the cannabis police. Actor Robert Mitchum was arrested for marijuana possession in 1948 and served 60 days in prison. Mitchum said: 'I'm ruined. I've been smoking reefers for years. I knew I would get caught sooner or later.' However, having served his time, he later joked: 'It was the first vacation I've had in seven years, like Palm Springs without the riff-raff.' In 1976 actor Ryan O'Neal fell foul of California's new dope laws when police found 140g (5oz) of cannabis in his Beverly Hills home. He was freed on bail on the understanding that he sought psychiatric help. Woody Harrelson, star of *Cheers*, was arrested but later released after planting four industrial hemp seeds on his property in Kentucky in 1998. 'We're facing a severe worldwide fibre shortage,' he explained. Meanwhile celebrity drugs guru Dr Timothy Leary was sentenced to ten years in jail for transportation of marijuana in 1975. One joint was found in the vagina of his daughter Susan while they were driving from Texas to California. He was released in 1976. In 1999 actor Matthew McConaughey was found naked and playing the bongos with a marijuana bong next to him when police busted his house. After spending a night in jail, the drug paraphernalia charges were swiftly dropped after he agreed to pay a $50 (£35) for violating noise ordinances.

Sports stars are not immune to the temptations of a joint either. In 1986 England cricket star Ian Botham admitted he had smoked cannabis. The authorities banned him for eight weeks. Meanwhile teen tennis sensation Jennifer Capriati fell down to earth with a bump when she was busted for possession in 1994. No further action was taken after she agreed to enter a drug treatment centre. It did her good – she bounced back and became the game's number one women's player. And, shortly after the laid back world of snowboarding hailed a new hero when Ross Rebagliati won the sport's first ever Olympic gold in 1998, he became a *cause célèbre* among the dope-smoking fraternity when traces of marijuana were found in his blood. Rebagliati was first stripped of his medal, then reinstated after he explained that he had not been smoking himself but sitting beside some snowboarding pals who were. 'I'm definitely going to change my lifestyle,' Rebagliati told reporters. 'Unfortunately for you, I'm not going to change my friends. My friends are real. I'm going to stand behind them and support them. I'm not going to deviate from that. I might have to wear a gas mask from now on, but whatever.'

But when it comes to celebrity cannabis smokers, they don't get much more famous than the British Prince Harry. In 2001, the 17-year-old prince was forced to attend a drugs rehabilitation clinic at the request of his father, Prince Charles, after he admitted that he had taken cannabis on several occasions. Harry told his father that he took cannabis at a secret party at Highgrove, Prince Charles's Gloucestershire home, and on other occasions when he was as young as 16. Anxious to be seen to be doing the right thing, Charles swiftly arranged for Harry, who is third in line to the throne, to visit Featherstone Lodge rehabilitation centre, in Peckham, south London. Senior aides to Prince Charles said they hoped that the public and the media would look upon Prince Harry's admission and potential drug problem 'sympathetically'. One official said, 'Unfortunately, this is something that many parents have to go through at one time or another. We acknowledge that on several occasions last summer, Prince Harry experimented with cannabis. It is not that he had or has a serious problem, but he did take the drug.'

One of Harry's big nights out, in which he is alleged to have smoked dope, ended in an after hours-drinking session at the Rattlebone Inn in Sherston, Wiltshire, near Highgrove, during holidays in 2000. It was alleged that police were called after a mock fight in which Prince Harry was said to have called a French employee a 'fucking frog' and was ordered to leave the premises.

> 49 per cent of English teenagers say that they have tried cannabis, a level far higher than in any other western European country.

A less high-profile but equally embarrassing bust was that of William Straw, the 17-year-old son of the then Home Secretary, Jack Straw. William was nailed by the *Daily Mail* newspaper in 1997. A reporter, tipped off that Straw was selling cannabis, met him in a pub in Kennington, south London, and bought £10 ($14.50) of dope from him. He was arrested and appeared at the local police station with his father after the Crown Prosecution Service advised that a caution was the most appropriate action. 'William is now learning the lessons of this episode and he has my support in doing so,' Jack Straw said.

IT'S A GAS – CANNABIS, COMEDY AND COMICS

Every movement needs a standard bearer – and in the case of the pot-head brigade there were two. In the 1970s Cheech and Chong took every nuance of marijuana's laid back, spaced out culture and milked it for laughs on record and in the movies. It was funny – but a whole lot funnier if you happened to be smoking a huge joint at the time.

After several unsuccessful years as wannabe folk musicians in Los Angeles and Edmonton, Canada, Richard 'Cheech' Marin and Tommy Chong became a double act in 1970. Identifying that a rich vein of material could be mined out of the booming hippie movement they began performing dope-laced songs and sketches in nightclubs until eventually they were spotted by a record producer. Their 1972 debut album *Cheech And Chong* was a hit and was followed by several others, including *Big Bambu* and *Los Cochinos*. With tracks entitled 'Trippin' In Court' and 'Let's Make A Drug Deal', fans were left in no doubt that here was an act that talked their language – not to mention the fact they often inserted free strips of rolling paper in their album sleeves.

'When I first got turned onto pot, it was almost legal in the sense that no one really knew what it was, so no one really cared about it, especially in Canada,' Chong said. 'I remember smoking it behind this jazz club with the guys that turned me on, and the police came and searched the car for booze. And we were all laughing hysterically. They wanted to know what kind of tobacco that was, and we told them it was Italian tobacco.'

In 1978 the duo made their movie breakthrough in *Up In Smoke*, a frantic caper that proved to be a box-office smash. Several more movies followed but, although the pair retained a strong fan base, their wasted, hippie personas were becoming increasingly outdated in the cocaine-fuelled 1980s. Ironically in the 1990s, the fashion for 1970s retro – with the return of flares, disco and hip movies such as *Dazed And Confused* – sparked a mini-revival in their fortunes. For most aged hippies, however, Cheech and Chong remain a fond memory in the record collection.

While Cheech and Chong undoubtedly cashed in on the dope culture of the 1970s, they would admit a debt of gratitude to the equally popular explosion in underground comic books that began to appear at the same time. Indeed comic books have been described by some as the ideal literature of cannabis culture – easy to read, full of spaced out drawings and often hilariously funny. In particular, the *Fabulous Furry Freak Brothers* provided a blueprint for the kind of character Cheech and Chong would later commit to vinyl and celluloid. Created in 1970 by Gilbert Shelton, the Fabulous Freaks have been described as the stoned equivalent of the Keystone Cops. Their relentless search for narcotic release, usually with all manner of weird and wonderful paraphernalia, swiftly earned them a cult following. Indeed one episode saw the brothers being invited to judge the Third Annual Cannabis Cup. Needless to say, they ended up consuming most of the exhibits.

But the Freaks were not the first cartoon characters to be associated with dope. It is testament to the paranoia of US Federal Bureau of Narcotics chief Harry J Anslinger that in the 1930s he was convinced Popeye the Sailor was in fact a marijuana-munching fiend. Popeye's ability to gain superhuman strength through consuming spinach through his pipe fitted in perfectly with Anslinger's ideas about the cannabis menace. The fact that Popeye was also a sailor didn't help him; sailors were held responsible for the spread of cannabis from the east to 'civilized' countries such as Britain and the United States. Perhaps as a result of Anslinger's delusions, 'spinach' became a jazz industry code-word for cannabis – and the inspiration for a wicked little number called 'The Spinach Song', performed by Julia Lee And Her Boyfriends in dope-filled jazz clubs in New York in 1938.

A major influence on subsequent cannabis comics was Harvey Kurtzman, the founder of *MAD* magazine in the 1950s and creator of the saucy Little Annie Fannie cartoon series, which appeared in *Playboy* in the 1960s and 1970s. Kurtzman used Annie Fannie as a vehicle for his own beliefs about drugs – and in particular the legalization of cannabis. He frequently allowed his characters to pontificate about the benefits of pot, and then showed them being ruthlessly beaten up by policemen who bore an uncanny resemblance to pigs.

Kurtzman provided the inspiration for Robert Crumb, regarded by most cannabis culture aficionados as the daddy of dope comics. Crumb, a prolific hash smoker, took Kurtzman's ideas and gave them a psychedelic twist. His series featuring Fritz the Cat and Mr Natural coincided with the hippie revolution of the late 1960s and not only used many of its cultural icons as their inspiration, but helped create many of them as well. It was Crumb's work that opened the door to Gilbert Shelton.

The man who encouraged and published not only Crumb and Shelton but a whole raft of hippie cartoonists was Denis Kitchen, himself a talented cartoonist who was the founder of the legendary Kitchen Sink Press. Kitchen Sink in turn spawned the likes of Rip Off Press and Last Gasp Press, which gave the world such characters as Harold Hedd, a dope-smoking macho man, and Dr Atomic, who gave readers advice on how to roll the perfect 'doobie'.

'We knew that comics were stultified, largely puerile, and unimaginative, and it was impossible to use the medium with any sense of real freedom and exploration,' Kitchen said. 'Those of us who considered ourselves hippies caught up in the anti-war movement and – yes – smoking pot, just looked at the world in a very different way. And comic books were a part of that world that we questioned. There was an immediate connection between going to buy your rolling papers at a head shop and going to get your comics. That was a natural alliance and I think a lot of people considered getting high and reading underground comics a natural thing to do.'

When the US government decided to clamp down on drug culture in the 1970s, one of their chosen methods was to use comic books. In 1971, the FBI contacted Stan Lee – creator of Marvel Comics and superheroes like Spider-Man – and asked him to create a story telling the dangers of drug addiction. Lee agreed, and later that year Spidey was seen preventing a junked-up black man from attempting to fly from the top of a tall building. Even as recently as 1999, Spidey was still promoting the anti-cannabis message. In a special four-parter, one of the characters is a pot-head movie star who smokes dope and then goes dancing on steel girders, encouraging his sappy fans to do the same. In 2000, both Marvel's Spider-Man and DC Comics' Batman received White House awards for their continued vigilance against the drug menace.

WWW.DOPE.COM – HASH ON THE NET

The advent of the Internet has allowed cannabis and its users unprecedented mainstream access. A growing number of dedicated sites now enable cannabis users across the globe the opportunity to discuss anything from medical issues, cooking recipes and different laws to advanced growing techniques and where to buy it. More importantly,

Packets of cannabis seeds for sale in a market in Amsterdam. Cultivation of cannabis is illegal in many countries, although it has been decriminalized in the Netherlands.

The cannabis plants seen here in an illegal nursery are of the skunk variety, a particularly potent form of the plant with a high THC content.

the authorities are increasingly aware that the Net has become a major outlet for dealers.

Not only is it possible to purchase different types of seeds and hydroponic devices (see p136), Internet users can now buy their own grass and have it delivered within a couple of days to their homes. For those frustrated by draconian laws against medical use, or those who simply enjoy the convenience of shopping for their drugs online, the Net is a positive boon.

Finding retail sites is not straightforward. Buying cannabis online is illegal and dealers are well aware of the increased interest of international drug squads. But, by the same token, clamping down on Internet drug sales is almost impossible – especially if the sellers come from countries, like Holland, where the laws are relaxed. Many sites are disguised as the websites of Amsterdam coffee shops. After ordering, customers are sent an email with an address on it and instructions to send cash. One Amsterdam dealer recently admitted to sending out over 1,000 packages a week to online clients across the world, and estimates that 99 per cent of the marijuana he sends out makes it through customs to the addresses intact. Usually it is sent in plastic zipper bags placed inside padded envelopes. While there is always a possibility that customs will intercept your parcel and come round to your house, this is so remote that most people are confident of taking the risk.

Some, however, are not convinced. 'We have run several messages on our website saying that one of the stupidest things you can do is buy pot through the Internet. It's even riskier than going up to somebody in the street,' says John Holmstrom, multimedia director for *High Times* magazine. 'Who knows who's behind the website? What if it's a government agency and they're keeping a list of everyone they're sending pot to?'

The cannabis seed trade is flourishing, both because the tiny, odourless seeds are easy to ship and because selling seeds is far more profitable than actual marijuana. Many seed sites are based in Holland and Canada, where possession of seeds is legal. The sites are places where global cannabis connoisseurs can compare notes or where novices can absorb pages and pages of free advice on cultivation.

RAGE AGAINST THE MACHINE – POT-HEADS FIGHT BACK

Increasingly what defines the culture of cannabis today is not so much the self-effacing placidity of the 1960s and 1970s, but a real sense of injustice and anger. It's as if cannabis, sick of being the butt of the joke and the sole territory of spaced-out hippies in flares and kaftans, is determined to be taken seriously.

'When I think of all the skulking around I've done, simply so I can have a nice joint in peace, it seems absolutely ludicrous,' says motor retailer Gareth Burns, 31. 'This is the 21st century, for Christ's sake. It's not as if I'm running around with an Uzi. I've never done anybody any harm in my life.'

In June 2000, charity worker Jerry Ham was busted with 3g of cannabis in his possession. Ham chose to contest the charge in front of a judge and jury. By doing this, he became one of a growing number of cannabis enthusiasts who are no longer prepared to take a slap on the wrist, a probable fine and caution and, more importantly, a criminal record that can be seen by potential employers and be raised in court should offenders face a charge on another occasion.

The number of those dealt with by the police in the UK for drugs offences involving cannabis doubled from 40,194 in 1990 to 86,034 in 1997 after Michael Howard announced that he was tripling the maximum fines.

Two recent developments are behind the new wave of people standing up for their rights to take cannabis. First, the changed public perception towards cannabis has seen a number of high-profile cannabis busts thrown out of court. Second, the legal labyrinth of the Human Rights Act, which was introduced in 2000 to prevent European governments from unduly interfering in the private life of an individual.

Jerry Ham pleaded not guilty, despite admitting possession, on the grounds that it should not be a crime. He argued that the amount of hash he possessed – less than 2g – was so small that prosecution amounted to a 'disproportionate and therefore unlawful response'. Calling for his case to be dismissed because it infringed his human rights, his case was backed by Liberty, the human rights campaign group.

His case mirrored that of 21-year-old labourer Daniel Westlake, who, when caught with a small amount of cannabis, refused to accept a caution and pleaded not guilty under the Human Rights Act. At time of writing, his case was due to come before the Court of Appeal, which has the power to declare the Misuse of Drugs Act incompatible with the Human Rights Act.

In America, meanwhile, a group called the Oakland Cannabis Buyers' Co-operative took their case for being allowed possession of the weed all the way to the Supreme Court - where, in a landmark ruling in 2001, all eight judges ruled that possession of cannabis was an offence in the United States whatever the circumstances. US Attorney General John Ashcroft hailed the ruling as 'a victory for the enforcement of our nation's drug laws'.

Sadly for Jerry Ham, his bid foundered at the first hurdle, when Judge Rivlin ruled his case should go ahead, saying that courts could only stay trials in exceptional circumstances, where the defendant could not receive a fair trial or where it was integral to the public interest that the trial should not take place. To accept that it should be widened to take into account 'proportionateness' under the Human Rights Act would be 'very wide and dangerously vague'. The judge said: 'The restriction of his right to take drugs in the privacy of his own home is not an intrusion on his personal space or an affront to his personality.' He added: 'No one would wish to stifle debate - nothing could be more healthy. If the defendant and his supporters wish to secure a change in the law, it can be achieved and must be done by normal democratic means. Until there is a change in the law, judges must continue to uphold it.'

Despite a clear direction to convict Ham in the judge's summing up, the jury of seven men and five women took two and a half hours to reach a 10-2 majority verdict of guilty. And Ham was sentenced to just two years conditional discharge.

Cannabis culture has, for over a century in the UK, been a culture of persecution. In 1998, the number of people in the UK given lifetime criminal records for cannabis offences passed the one million mark. The annual number is in excess of 100,000 - more than 90 per cent for personal use. In the USA, the number of convictions tops one million annually.

But, as so often, the statistics mask a number of sad stories - like that of TV cameraman Brian Lace, who was caught in possession of a small amount of cannabis and fined £200 ($290). With a criminal record to his name, Lace suddenly found that he was sacked from his job, evicted from his house and had his car repossessed. Unable to find work after a year of living on benefits in a bedsit, he could take it no longer and hanged himself from the back of a door.

But a more typical scenario is that of the multiple sclerosis sufferer who accepted a police caution for smoking cannabis, not realizing that by doing so she was giving herself a criminal record for life. She only discovered this when she applied for a visa to visit the USA and was refused entry on account of her 'criminal' past. Or the bakery manager whose insurance company refused to pay up after a burglary because he had a criminal record from an earlier cannabis caution.

When one former electrician was caught with 43g- (1½oz) worth, he was prosecuted for possession and intent to supply, a charge he denies. He spent 11 weeks in jail and 60 days wearing an electronic tag. 'Society has basically written me off,' he says. 'As a cannabis user who has never hurt anyone, I am put in the same category as rapists and robbers.'

HISTORY

> 'Early man experimented with all plant materials that he could chew and could not have avoided discovering the properties of cannabis, for in his quest for seeds and oil he certainly ate the sticky tops of the plant. Upon eating hemp for the euphoric, ecstatic and hallucinatory aspects may have introduced man to an other-worldly plane from which emerged religious beliefs, perhaps even the concept of deity. The plant became accepted as a special gift of the gods, a sacred medium for communion with the sacred world and as such it has remained in some cultures to the present.' – From *Man And Marijuana*, Richard E. Schultes, 1967

IN THE BEGINNING

Blame the ancient medicine men. If it hadn't been for them and their infernal meddling, *cannabis sativa*, an otherwise unremarkable species of hemp plant, would have remained just what its name means in Latin: useful hemp. Its tough stalk would have been used for the production of rope and durable textiles such as 'canvas' sails, its edible seeds would have been used for food, its pulp for fuel and paper and its oil as a base for paints and varnishes.

But no. Because cannabis is also a herb, it attracted the attention of shamen, soothsayers, and witch doctors – all of whom were eager to explore the therapeutic properties of its leaves, buds and flowers.

The Chinese medicine men proved to be particularly good pharmacists. As soon as they discovered that various tinctures of cannabis were therapeutic, it was only a matter of time before they realised that, in greater quantities, it was highly narcotic. Around 2600 BC, they began getting stoned on a regular basis and, from that moment, the impact of cannabis on the culture of mankind was to be seismic.

It was Herodotus, the Greek historian, who first recorded the psychedelic effects of cannabis during his travels through northern Europe in 430 BC. Before that, the plant had cropped up in various ancient pharmacopoeia, including that of the Hindus in India in around 1200 BC, in which it was described as 'sacred grass' and recommended as an offering to Shiva – and, some 500 years later, in the *Zend-Avesta*, a sacred Persian text that lists more than 10,000 medicinal plants.

> More than 300,000 people are searched in the street in the UK each year by police looking for drugs.

Herodotus came across cannabis for the first time while in Scythia, in what is now northern Asia. He was mightily impressed with what he saw: 'There is in that country kannabis growing both wild and cultivated,' he wrote in his *Histories*. 'Fuller and taller than flax, the Thracians use it to make garments very like linen. The Scythians take kannabis seed...and throw it on the red hot stones. It smoulders and sends up suck billows of steam smoke that no Greek vapour bath can surpass it. The Scythians howl with joy in these vapour baths – which serve them instead of bathing, for they never wash their bodies with water.'

By AD 70, cannabis had been appropriated from the heathens of Scythia and was commonplace in the civilized ancient world. Another Greek historian, Dioscorides, observed that tinctures and poultices made from the leaves of the plant were very popular among physicians in Rome who used them for a number of treatments, but primarily as a painkiller. Within 150 years, however, the Roman historian Galen noted another, more familiar use of the plant at social occasions. 'It is customary,' he wrote, 'to give hemp to guests to promote hilarity and enjoyment.'

There can be little doubt that cannabis was taken to Rome by the many eastern merchants and travellers who passed through that most cosmopolitan of ancient cities. Certainly it was the east that provided the most ideal climatic conditions for cultivating the plant, and it was there that the hot-bed of cannabis production and use were consolidated. In AD

800, the prophet Mohammed gave the thumbs up to cannabis use among his disciples, while at the same time prohibiting the consumption of alcohol.

Indeed, right up until the Middle Ages, society's relationship with cannabis was blissfully content. It was used for medicine and for recreation in equal measure, and there was certainly none of the angst that typified later attitudes to the drug. What seems to have driven the first wedge was the fact that cannabis was so firmly associated with the east and, in particular, the religions of the east.

In 1484, Pope Innocent VIII labelled cannabis as 'an unholy sacrament of the Satanic mass' and issued a papal ban on cannabis medicines – this was perhaps one of the first recorded instances of anti-cannabis legislation (although 50 years earlier Ottoman Emir Soudoun Scheikhouni had banned the eating of cannabis).

In the west, the importance of cannabis – or more particularly hemp – was not as a medicine or narcotic. In 16th-century Britain, an island whose might had been largely built upon its navy, hemp was an invaluable source of tough, durable fibre that was used to make sails. Henry VIII went so far as to order every farmer in the land to devote a quarter acre out of every 60 to the cultivation of hemp plants, or face a hefty fine of three shillings and fourpence. To his daughter, Elizabeth I, beleaguered by the Spanish for much of her reign, the hemp plant was even more important. Under an edict issued by her in 1563, farmers were ordered to grow it or face a whopping £5 ($7.25) fine. On mainland Europe, meanwhile,

> The Commons Select Committee on Drug Policy recommended downgrading cannabis from class B to class C, abolishing jail for cannabis possession, and treating small, personal supplies of cannabis plants as simple possession.

Elizabeth's nemesis Philip of Spain was also aware of the importance of hemp and ordered it to be grown in his colonies as far afield as Argentina and Oregon.

In the 17th century, the popularity of cannabis as a medicine made a comeback among western doctors. In 1653, the English physician Nicholas Culpeper claimed it 'allayeth inflammations, easeth the pain of gout, tumours or knots of joints, pain of hips'. Indeed, in Europe, the idea of smoking the plant for purposes of recreation appears not to have crossed anyone's mind. Tobacco was the drug of choice but even that was frowned upon by the majority.

This was not the case in the Middle East and Asia, where pot smoking had reached epidemic proportions, especially among the poorer classes. Napoleon was reportedly horrified by the scale of cannabis use among the locals when he arrived in Egypt in 1798. He was even more put out when, despite banning his own soldiers from partaking, the pastime arrived back in Paris with them and was enthusiastically adopted by the French lower classes. It was not long before Napoleon's troops were followed by eastern dealers eager to tap into new markets in Europe.

Hash had arrived in the west with a vengeance. No longer was it regarded simply as a medicine or as a source of fibre for making sails. Here was a powerful narcotic, cheaply available to those with hard lives and little money who wanted to get off their heads, and overpoweringly exotic to society dandies and intellectuals who had suddenly acquired a new and exciting way of spending their evenings.

For the next 200 years the humble cannabis plant was to become the centre of a whole new world, one which was embraced by some and despised by others. And, even today, it is a world in which the two sides still refuse to meet.

Near the Punjab and Pab, in Sutlej and Sind,
Where the cobras-di-capello abound,
Where the poppy, palm, and the tamarind,
With cummin and ginger festoon the ground –
And the capsicum fields are all abloom,
From the hills above to the vales below,
Entrancing the air with a rich perfume,
There too does the greenish Cannabis grow:
Inflaming the blood with the living fire,
Till the burning joys like the eagles rise,
And the pulses throb with strange desires,
While passion awakes with a wild surprise:-
O to eat that drug, and to dream all day.
Of the maids that live by the Bengal Bay!

'A Hasheesh Sonnet' by Victor Robinson, 1910

Across the world, cannabis has inspired such mass outbreaks of judicial schizophrenia, public outcry, religious zeal and general hopeless dithering that even today, 4,700 years since it was first used, it appears that governments still haven't got the foggiest idea of what to do with the humble *cannabis sativa* plant.

DAZED AND CONFUSED – CANNABIS IN THE USA

Few countries have had such an angst-ridden relationship with cannabis as the USA. Indeed at one stage, in the 1930s, the country was gripped by such paranoia about the deleterious effects of the weed that it seemed the population as a whole was on a communal bad trip.

Yet, within 30 years, America was responsible for raising the cultural profile of marijuana to iconic status. The peace and free love movement in the 1960s was largely fuelled by cannabis; the Woodstock festival in 1969 was its culmination and the conflict in Vietnam is remembered largely as a war fought under the influence of drugs.

Cannabis – or rather hemp – was originally a godsend to the pioneers of the New World. The likes of George Washington and Thomas Jefferson not only encouraged farmers to grow the plant in order to make durable and versatile hemp fibre, they grew it themselves.

But by the middle part of the 19th century, as the commercial value of cannabis fell, it became clear to the establishment that the plant's stock as a narcotic was rising. From the hashish houses of cosmopolitan Paris and London, word soon reached the east coast US cultural intelligentsia, who became eager devotees and experimenters. New York began to set up its own fashionable hash houses and attendance there became *de rigueur* among the well-heeled and open-minded bright young things.

Of these, none was more devoted to 'hasheesh' than Fitz Hugh Ludlow (1837–70), well-to-do son of a respectable New York minister who, in his 34 short years, consumed the drug in heroic quantities and reported its mind-bending effects in a series of first-hand accounts, the most famous being *The Hasheesh Eater* in 1856.

'I had caught a glimpse through the chinks of my earthly prison of the immeasurable sky, which should one day overarch me with unconceived sublimity of view, and resound in my ear with unutterable music,' Ludlow writes. 'A shock, as of some unimagined vital force, shoots without warning through my entire frame, leaping to my fingers' ends, piercing my brain, startling me till I nearly spring from my chair.'

It is worth noting that Ludlow and his fellow hasheesh pioneers were experimenting with cannabis in its purest and strongest form. They were, literally, eating it. And while their accounts of spaced-out hash houses, psychedelic trips and spiritual uncaging fascinated the public, it was little more than titillation, comparable perhaps to the acid-fuelled ramblings of modern American drug experimentalists such as Timothy Leary and Hunter S Thompson.

Cannabis the drug was a middle-class fad and therefore, in the eyes of middle-class American establishment, it did not present a threat. In the 1870s, however, things began to change. It was around this time that recreational use of cannabis cigarettes began to spread like wildfire in the New World, particularly among impoverished labourers in the Caribbean, Brazil, and Central America who sought a hangover-free escape from their backbreaking work in the fields. By the turn of the century, the pastime had spread across the border into the USA, by way of migrant workers and soldiers. Initially it took hold in the Deep South, manifesting itself particularly in New Orleans where it had a clear effect on early jazz musicians who tried to recapture in their music the inhibitions they felt while under the influence of marijuana.

As its use became more widespread across the country, the anxiety of white America became increasingly palpable. Cannabis became associated with the unspeakable underclasses – the blacks, the poor and the Mexicans. Reports from over the border told of violent ne'er-do-wells like Pancho Villa, the Mexican revolutionary whose army regularly smoked 'marijuana' (Mexican for 'intoxicant') to give them courage for battle. Folk songs like 'La Cucaracha' – written about one of Villa's marijuana-starved 'cockroaches', or foot soldiers – were the first examples of the subject of cannabis entering the mainstream of popular culture.

> La cucaracha, la cucaracha
> Ya no puede caminar
> Porque no tiene, porque no tiene
> Marihuana que fumar

This translates as: 'The cockroach, the cockroach/Can no longer walk/Because he hasn't, because he hasn't/Marijuana to smoke.'

(This, incidentally, is also the origin of the word 'roach', a nickname for a marijuana cigarette butt.)

By the 1920s, America had already passed Prohibition laws banning alcohol, so it was no surprise that marijuana was the next to feel the weight of the puritanical establishment. In 1923 the drug was outlawed in New Orleans and, by the end of the Prohibition era in 1933, 17 states had banned cannabis. But while alcohol made a welcome return to the speakeasies, one man was embarking upon a personal crusade to vilify cannabis. It was a campaign that was, ironically, to raise the profile of what was still a little-known drug into its present status.

Harry J Anslinger was an ambitious bureaucrat who first made his name in the 1920s as a fervent Prohibitionist, chasing rum runners out of the American consulate in the West Indies. When, in 1930, the American government was looking for someone to head up its newly created Federal Bureau of Narcotics, Anslinger was the obvious choice. Anslinger set about his new job with a gusto that bordered on the fanatical. As far as he was concerned cannabis was Public Enemy Number One.

In July, a *Guardian*/ICM poll found that 65 per cent of the public agreed that prosecution for cannabis should be the lowest priority for the police.

More than 70 years after the arrival of the first hash houses, private cannabis establishments were still highly popular in 1930s New York. Known as 'tea pads', they were as secretive and illicit as opium dens and were set up by mutual arrangement in inconspicuous apartment rooms predominantly in the Harlem area. But instead of emaciated addicts, those who regularly frequented tea pads were refined marijuana aficionados, usually of high social standing, who enjoyed sampling different blends of the drug in a manner similar to tea tasters. 'The only illumination in Chappy's place was a blue bulb glowing in a glass case of the slot machine phonograph,' a report in *The New Yorker* in 1938 described. 'All tea pads, or marijuana joints, use the blue lamps and nickel machines to induce and sustain the hashish mood.'

The LaGuardia Report into American cannabis use in 1944 regarded the inhabitants of Tea Pads rather as though they were some strange alien life form. 'The marijuana smoker derives greater satisfaction if he is smoking in the presence of others. His attitude in the "tea-pad" is that of a relaxed individual, free from the anxieties and cares of the realities of life. The "tea-pad" takes on the atmosphere of a very congenial social club... A constant observation was the extreme willingness to share and puff on each other's cigarettes.'

Anslinger's response to what he saw as a cancerous cannabis sub-culture eating away at the heart of America was not to clamp down with police raids as he had done during Prohibition. Instead, he issued a series of scabrous anti-cannabis articles in magazines and newspapers. Without doubt the best known is his 1937 diatribe, *Marijuana: Assassin Of Youth*.

Here indeed is the unknown quantity among narcotics. No one can predict its effect. No one knows, when he places a marijuana cigarette to his lips, whether he will become a joyous reveler in a musical heaven, a mad insensate, a calm philosopher, or a murderer. That youth has been selected by the peddlers of this poison as an especially fertile field makes it a problem of serious concern to every man and woman in America.

It would be well for law-enforcement officers everywhere to search for marijuana behind cases of criminal and sex assault. During the last year a young male addict was hanged in Baltimore for criminal assault on a ten-year-old girl. His defence was that he was temporarily insane from smoking marijuana. In Alamosa, Colorado, a degenerate brutally attacked a young girl while under the influence of the drug. In Chicago, two marijuana-smoking boys murdered a policeman. In at least two dozen other comparatively recent cases of murder or degenerate sex attacks, many of them committed by youths, marijuana proved to be a contributing cause.'

Anslinger concluded:

Therein lies much of the cruelty of marijuana, especially in its attack upon youth. The young, immature brain is a thing of impulses,

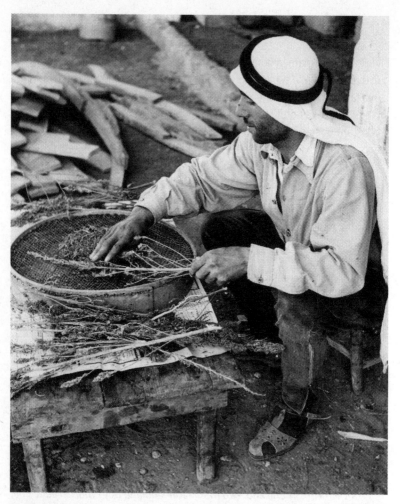

Some farmers separate the resin from the cannabis flower by rubbing them between their hands, producing a form of the drug called *hashish* in Arabic. Here, a Lebanese man rubs the plants against a screen to shake loose the dope.

Blocks of hashish (FOREGROUND), leaves, and flowering tops of the hemp plant *Cannabis sativa*. The hashish is heated, then crumbled into tobacco in a hand-rolled cigarette. The leaves and flowering tops can be used like tobacco and smoked, imbibed as a tea, or eaten in food. When smoked (as a joint or reefer), the effects of the drug can be felt within a few minutes.

Cannabis-smoking equipment. In the matchbox (TOP LEFT) are some dried leaves from the *Cannabis sativa* plant. These are smoked in a pipe (CENTRE RIGHT) or rolled with tobacco into a joint (UPPER CENTRE). Also pictured is square of cannabis resin or *black* (CENTRE LEFT), a more concentrated form of the drug, which is heated and crumbled into a pipe or joint.

upon which the 'unknown quantity' of the drug acts as an almost overpowering stimulant. In New Orleans, of 437 persons of varying ages arrested for a wide range of crimes, 125 were addicts. Of 37 murderers, 17 used marijuana, and of 193 convicted thieves, 34 were 'on the weed'. This means a job of unceasing watchfulness by every police department and by every public-spirited civic organization. It calls for campaigns of education in every school, so that children will not be deceived by the wiles of peddlers, but will know of the insanity, the disgrace, the horror which marijuana can bring to its victim.

The effect on the American public of Anslinger's vivid propaganda was electrifying. In 1936 a movie was released entitled *Reefer Madness*, inspired almost totally by Anslinger's anti-cannabis tirades. Starring such C-movie names as Dave O'Brien, Lillian Miles, Dorothy Short and Carleton Young, the film depicted how one hit from a cannabis joint led its innocent young cast into insanity and death. Subtitled 'Marijuana: weed from the Devil's garden', and with such tag lines as 'One moment of bliss – a lifetime of regret' and 'Hunting a thrill, they inhaled a drag of concentrated sin', *Reefer Madness* bombed at the box office but remains a vivid example of the national cannabis frenzy Anslinger succeeded in stirring up in 1930s middle America.

Swept along on the mood of the nation, Anslinger succeeded in getting the Marijuana Tax Act passed through Congress in 1937. The law placed prohibitive taxes on cannabis – $1 (69p) per ounce (30g) for industrial or medical use and $100 (£69) per ounce (30g) for people using it for recreational purposes (with prison terms and hefty fines for transgressors) – and effectively outlawed it. The first person tried under the new laws was Samuel Caldwell of Colorado. Charged with selling a small amount of grass, he was sentenced to four years hard labour at the notorious Leavenworth Prison.

But Anslinger wasn't finished there. Once he had cannabis on the ground he was determined to keep kicking. In the 1940s, he turned his attention back to New Orleans and despatched agents to keep tabs on the thriving jazz scene and reefer-puffing exponents such as Louis Armstrong, Duke Ellington, Cab Calloway, Fats Waller and Jimmy Dorsey. 'At first you was a misdemeanour. But as the years rolled by you lost your "misde" and got meaner and meaner,' Louis Armstrong remarked acidly.

Anslinger continued his one-man crusade until 1961, when the Single Convention on Narcotic Drugs created an international commitment to unilateral war on drugs. Yet the 1960s proved to be the decade in which cannabis truly came of age as America's (and the rest of the world's) recreational drug of choice – and, ironically, responsibility for its popularity has been laid firmly on the shoulders of its arch enemy.

In an interview in 1974, just a year before Harry Anslinger's death, former deputy director of the Bureau of Narcotics and Dangerous Drugs, John Finlator, said: 'Before Harry Anslinger came along, the public didn't know anything about marijuana and they didn't care. They just believed what people told them. Particularly, the Mexican-Americans were using it, and we thought that was bad for a number of reasons. Racial bias was one of them. The last Harris Poll showed 70 per cent still against legalization. But asked how they felt about the new Oregon law, where marijuana is treated like a parking ticket, 36 per cent favoured it with 49 per cent opposed. So you can see the trend: decriminalization is coming soon.'

In the 1960s, marijuana use was so commonplace that even the President used it. In an article printed in *High Times* in 1974, an unnamed dealer with links to the White House wrote: 'Early one evening I received a telephone call at my apartment at Georgetown. It was one of JFK's most trusted Press liaisons, who informed me the President was planning a short vacation. He was taking his boat out with family and friends, and I was asked if I could provide him with the memos I had drawn up in accordance with our conversation two weeks earlier. Could I have everything ready by ten o'clock that night? I knew exactly what was meant by the call, because the President hadn't asked me to draw up any memos. By ten I had prepared a manila folder full of blank paper. Inside was an ounce [30g] of fresh Panamanian.'

Within a year of the UN Single Convention and the retirement of Harry Anslinger, President John F Kennedy – who was rumoured to smoke marijuana for pleasure as well as a cure for chronic back pain – had ordered a study into the nation's narcotic problem and this produced some startling results. Not only, it concluded, had the hazards of marijuana been 'exaggerated', but the harsh criminal penalties for recreational users (which by 1961 in Georgia included the death penalty for being caught selling twice to a minor), were 'in poor social perspective'. Within a year, Congress was passing laws that made a clear distinction between cannabis and hard drugs.

In his retirement home in Pennsylvania, Harry Anslinger must have been in despair as he watched 30 years of hard work crumble to dust almost overnight. But John Finlator was right – by oppressing cannabis so vehemently, Anslinger had merely served to make the younger generation insanely curious to try it out. Not only had cannabis proved to be a benign assassin of youth, but that youth had now grown up and taken Anslinger's place. And just as cannabis had provided the early jazz musicians with inspiration, so the drug was enthusiastically embraced by pop musicians in the 1960s. 'We were smoking marijuana for breakfast,' the late John Lennon recalled, while Bob Dylan explained his cannabis philosophy: 'Now these things aren't drugs. They just bend your mind a little. I think everybody's mind should be bent once in a while.'

Dylan first got the taste for marijuana as a student in Minnesota and then set about introducing it to many of the leading musicians of the day, including The Beatles. By the late 1960s, cannabis was as much a part of any self-respecting pop star's accoutrements as his/her guitar.

Ironically, while musicians urged everyone to make love not war, it was the conflict in Vietnam that cemented marijuana use among millions of young Americans. The battlefields of southeast Asia were also a source of cheap and plentiful grass and, to the chagrin of the US Army's generals, thousands of conscripts turned to the drug as a means of blotting out the horrors of the war. It is thought that as many as 75 per cent of the soldiers sent to Vietnam smoked cannabis at some point.

Back home, cannabis use exploded, its cause championed by high-profile figures like the beat poet Allen Ginsberg, who campaigned vociferously for its legalization. 'The actual experience of the smoked herb has been clouded by a fog of dirty language perpetrated by a crowd of fakers who have not had the experience and yet insist on downgrading it,' Ginsberg pronounced in 1965. In 1969, *Life* magazine reported that as many as 12 million Americans had tried pot. Even this was a conservative estimate.

The final nail in the coffin of Harry Anslinger's anti-cannabis crusade came in 1970 when the American government declared his Marijuana Tax Act unconstitutional. In truth, Congress was belatedly reacting to the untrammelled rise in the drug's popularity during the 1960s. As the new decade dawned, millions of middle-class Americans were openly flaunting Anslinger's arcane laws and the police were largely turning a blind eye. In the White House, President Richard Nixon declared he was against the legalization of pot, but in 1973 ordered the Shafer Commission to take a fresh look into the subject. Its findings, like those

> The British Medical Association has stated, 'The acute toxicity of cannabinoids is extremely low – no deaths have been directly attributed to their recreational or therapeutic use.'

of Kennedy's commission 12 years earlier, were amazing. Not only did it recommend that people should be allowed to possess cannabis for personal use, it argued that selling or giving away small amounts of the weed was totally acceptable.

In the light of the Shafer Commission's report, Congress passed a raft of new cannabis laws. While not legalizing it, the government scrapped many of the punitive minimum sentences and reclassified cannabis as a soft drug.

By the mid-1970s, an estimated 40 million Americans had tried pot. In a speech to Congress, President Jimmy Carter said: 'Penalties against possession of a drug should not be more damaging to an individual than the use of the drug itself. Nowhere is this more clear than in the laws against possession of marijuana in private for personal use.'

The speech, made 40 years after the American government's jack-booted clampdown on cannabis, was a watershed moment in the drug's history. For a brief moment, it seemed that the next logical step was to be the legalization of cannabis. Instead, the rug was about to be pulled from under cannabis's feet.

Less than ten years after the Federal government relaxed its anti-cannabis laws and commissions ordered by Presidents Nixon and Ford were advocating legalization, the drugs landscape in America had changed once again. Peace, love and understanding about cannabis had been replaced by guilt, fear and paranoia. The country was gripped by Reefer Madness all over again – only this time, the anti-marijuana backlash made Harry Anslinger's excessive campaign seem tame by comparison.

Where once first-time marijuana offenders could expect nothing more than a fine, they now faced the prospect of anything from probation to life imprisonment and their property was seized indiscriminately. Even people found carrying drug paraphernalia, such as pipes and roach clips, could expect to land behind bars.

The dramatic sea-change of opinion began to manifest itself in the late 1970s. In the heartland of America, the conservative majority railed against what they perceived as betrayal by the liberal government in Washington. The medical and legal debate about cannabis had, they believed, clouded the moral issue. What sort of a country were they living in when 1 in 12 high school students confessed to smoking pot on a daily basis? Soon, concerned parents were setting up anti-pot groups all over the USA. They eventually amalgamated into the National Federation of Parents for Drug Free Youth.

Conservative politicians were not slow to jump on the bandwagon. Ronald Reagan sailed into the White House on a rabid anti-drugs ticket. In 1982 he created the White House Drug Abuse Policy Office and, over the next six years, set about reinstating all the old marijuana laws. His successor, George Bush, continued the clampdown with equal relish and by the end of the 1980s it was estimated that America had spent an astonishing $3 billion (£2 billion) on its anti-drugs war.

The arrival of Democrat Bill Clinton in the White House was initially viewed with hope by the pro-cannabis lobby. After all, here, for the first time since Kennedy, was a young president. Even better, he was a baby boomer and a draft dodger. Surely Clinton of all people would signal an easier ride for the weed. They were to be sorely disappointed. Although Clinton admitted he had smoked cannabis, he also famously pointed out he did not inhale. It was a blatant cop out and a bitter blow to those who regarded him as the saviour of marijuana. In 1997, over 700,000 people were arrested for marijuana-related offences. Harry Anslinger couldn't have asked for more.

In 1973, Anslinger's anti-cannabis missionary work was taken over by the newly formed Drugs Enforcement Administration (DEA). This is hardly surprising, since the DEA's lineage can be traced back directly to the Prohibition bureaux of the 1920s and 1930s, from which Anslinger first emerged.

Anslinger would have been pleased with his progeny. Far from mellowing in their stance towards cannabis, the DEA hardened it. But instead of the rabid diatribes and scaremongering so beloved by Harry J, the DEA had the weight of some pretty punitive laws behind them. Traffickers, in particular, could expect little or no mercy if caught in the act by agency operatives: the penalty for being caught trafficking 1,000kg (2,200lb) or 1,000 cannabis plants was a jail term of at least ten years. And that was just for a first offence. If caught twice, offenders could look forward to 20 years or more behind bars. Even punters caught dealing amounts of 50kg (110lb) faced a sentence of up to five years for a first offence.

The DEA definitely saw the cannabis scenario in terms of black and white, with no shades of grey in between. Indeed, they showed their colours very early in their existence. In 1973, they were petitioned to reclassify marijuana as a Schedule II drug that could be prescribed by physicians. The matter took no less than 13 years to come to public hearing stage, and even then the hearings lasted two years. Despite the DEA's legal expert recommending rescheduling, and his conclusions that 'cannabis is one of the safest therapeutically active substances known to man', the DEA denied the petition. As far as the DEA are concerned, the marijuana problem among America's youth is rife – and they have extensive research to prove it, as their own literature proclaims: 'According to a survey conducted by Phoenix House, drug abuse treatment and research organization, marijuana was the drug of choice for 87 per cent of teenagers entering treatment programmes in New York during the first quarter of 1999. A national survey conducted in 1996 revealed that 83 per cent of teenagers in treatment perceived, at one time or another, marijuana to be less dangerous than other illicit drugs, and 60 per cent agreed that using marijuana made it easier for them to consume other drugs, including cocaine, methamphetamine, and LSD.

Similar statistics were found by the 1999 Monitoring the Future study, which showed that marijuana is the illegal drug most frequently used by young people. Among high school seniors, 49.7 per cent reported using marijuana at least once in their lives. By comparison, that figure was 41.7 per cent for seniors in 1995 and 32.6 per cent in 1992. The 1999 NHSDA (National Household Survey of Drug Abuse) found that nearly one in 13 youths aged 12–17 were current users of marijuana in 1999 and that the prevalence of marijuana use among youth more than doubled from 1992 to 1999. The 1998 National Centre on Addiction and Substance Abuse study indicates that adolescents are first exposed and try marijuana at a very young age. According to the study, '50 per cent of 13 year olds reported that they could find and purchase marijuana, and 49 per cent of teens surveyed said that they first tried marijuana at age 13 or younger.' Armed with such damning research, the DEA's philosophy has been disarmingly simple: Kids are taking marijuana, therefore marijuana must be destroyed at all costs.

Recognizing that dope is about the only commonly used narcotic grown within the borders of the USA, in 1979 the DEA initiated the Domestic Cannabis Eradication and Suppression Program aimed at stamping out the cultivation of the cannabis plant. At first, plantations in Hawaii and California were targeted, and the operation saw some initial success. In Hawaii, for example, the DEA claim to have dried up the marijuana supply on the islands and forced traffickers to smuggle from the mainland. By 1985, the operation had spread to all 50 US states and in 2000 the DEA redoubled their efforts by spending $13 million (£9 million) to support the 96 state and local agencies in their aggressive eradication enforcement. In 1999 alone, the DEA claimed to have eradicated over 3.5 million cultivated cannabis plants, securing 12,000 arrests, the seizure of 3,700 weapons and the appropriation of $27 million (£18.5 million) in illegal assets.

In 20 years the operation has, according to the DEA, 'curbed the availability of domestically grown marijuana and...caused the outdoor cultivators to abandon larger outdoor plots for the safety and concealment of smaller, indoor cultivating areas.' But it has also landed the Agency with a new headache. Forced from their fields, dope growers are now turning to sophisticated indoor growing techniques, such as computerized irrigation and hydroponic cultivation – the cultivation of plants in nutrient solution rather than soil. Hydroponic cultivation, incidentally, not only makes it easier for growers to clandestinely cultivate marijuana indoors but it also enables them to produce extremely potent marijuana.

Not to be outdone, the DEA and its co-operating agencies have set about employing equally advanced technology to wage war against the marijuana growers. One such technique is thermal imaging, which identifies indoor cultivation by detecting the signature heat from lighting used to grow the plants.

The DEA are also aware that their efforts to clamp down on home-grown hash meant that, like the Hawaiians, traffickers in the US are increasingly looking to import the drug from abroad, in particular from South America. Kilos of cannabis chug across the southern US border concealed in false compartments, fuel tanks, seats and tyres of private and commercial vehicles, pickup trucks, vans, mobile homes and horse trailers. Larger shipments (up to multi-thousand kilogram amounts), are smuggled in tractor-trailer trucks in false compartments and among legitimate bulk shipments, such as agricultural products. In 1997, a record 593 tonnes/tons of marijuana was seized along the southwest border in 1997 – approximately 25 per cent more than that seized in 1996 and nearly double that seized in 1995.

As a result, the smugglers, however, have now turned to more traditional routes into the US, using cargo vessels, pleasure boats and fishing boats to sail up the coast of Mexico, either to US ports or drop off sites along the US coast and the Bahamas.

DOPE FIELDS – GREEN PLAINS AS FAR AS THE EYE CAN SEE

From his position in the passenger seat of the helicopter, Wise County Sheriff Ronnie Oakes could see for miles across the West Virginia countryside, almost to the Kentucky border in the distance. But, as the helicopter swooped low over the vast tracts of remote farmland

and up towards the Appalachians, Sheriff Oakes saw something that made his eyes pop out.

Below him, on the site of a long-abandoned coal mine, was a stunningly verdant landscape consisting of over 4,000 marijuana plants, some as tall as 3.5m (10ft). Oakes, working for the Virginia National Guard under the auspices of the DEA, had been hoping to find some evidence of marijuana cultivation during his routine surveillance flight over Wise County. What he had discovered was one of the biggest plantations of the drug he had ever seen, and certainly the largest in Virginia's history.

'It's so distant and remote, they thought no one would ever find it,' Oakes said. 'We'd find one patch, then another, then another. I've never seen so much marijuana in my life.'

The episode, in August 2000, provides a typical example of the methods of the hash growers, and the ruthless slash and burn policy the DEA have adopted in their single-minded quest to obliterate cannabis cultivation in the US.

Growing on the plantation was nearly 2 tonnes/tons of cannabis, with an estimated street value of $8 million (£5.5 million). The site was so remote that police had to haul the plants out by helicopter. Tracks and campsites in the area indicated that the growers had to take all-terrain vehicles part of the way before hiking to their crop.

Authorities from Wise County, the National Guard and the Virginia State Police spent three days cutting, baling and hauling the illegal crop. Then a crowd of locals gathered at the Wise County landfill to watch police burn and bury the plants. 'A lot of people were happy, but a few others probably weren't,' Oakes said.

According to the DEA, an estimated 40 per cent of the USA's marijuana supply comes from the Appalachian area that includes parts of Virginia and Kentucky. In Kentucky, for example, 500,000 plants were eradicated in 1999.

As the fragrant smoke curled into the Virginia sky, Sheriff Oakes remained sanguine. 'If they didn't have a market for it, they wouldn't be growing all these plants,' he told reporters. 'There's not much coal mining around here anymore, so I guess they'd thought they'd put the land to a different use.'

FIST OF IRON – GENERAL BARRY McCAFFREY

President Bill Clinton famously smoked a joint but never inhaled. Quite what General Barry McCaffrey made of the Chief Executive's admission remains a mystery – although it isn't hard to guess. During his four year reign as Clinton's director of the White House office of national drug control policy – in other words, the USA's drug tsar – McCaffrey earned himself a reputation as being a man who would quite happily drag anyone who so much as looked at a joint to the electric chair and flick the switch himself.

'There is not a single shred of evidence that shows that smoked marijuana is useful or needed,' he announced upon his appointment in 1996. 'This is not science. This is not medicine. This is a cruel hoax.'

To those old enough to remember, McCaffrey's words brought to mind a previous American drugs tsar – namely Harry J Anslinger. Certainly, within a few weeks of his appointment by Clinton, McCaffrey had laid out his stall in an equally uncompromising fashion. Responding to a claim by the American national institute of health that inhaled marijuana 'has the potential to improve chemotherapy-related nausea and vomiting', McCaffrey stated that 'marijuana is a gateway drug'. Meanwhile, he poured scorn on a US government criminal justice and drug policy sub-committee, claiming that they were the only people who backed drug reform in the US and, furthermore, were 'a carefully camouflaged, well-funded, tightly-knit core of people whose goal is to legalize drug use'.

He saved his most potent venom, however, for the Dutch, whose drugs policies are the most liberal in the world. 'The murder rate in Holland is double that in the United States, and the per capita crime rates are much higher than the United States,' he snarled. 'That's drugs.' When the Dutch ambassador to the USA responded that not only did McCaffrey's claims have no basis in fact because he had included attempted murders in his figures, and that in reality America's murder rate was four times as high, McCaffrey was not fazed in the slightest. Far from it. The figures, he argued, proved that 'the Dutch are a much more violent society and more inept at murders – and that's not much to brag about.'

The appointment of someone as hard line as McCaffrey by an administration as supposedly liberal as the Clinton's Democrats may at first seem confusing. But Clinton, acutely aware of his public image, was also very aware that his, 'I smoked but didn't inhale' tag was something of an albatross around his neck. More importantly, he did not wish to be perceived as a president who, after years of Republican zero tolerance towards drugs, let the country go wild by allowing them easier access to pot. In the US, the tide of opinion was increasingly turning in favour of cannabis as a legitimate medicine, largely thanks to organizations like the Lindesmith Center, a drug policy institute funded by billionaire financier George Soros. Its director, Ethan Nadelmann, summed up Lindesmith's philosophy when he said: 'Most drug policy reformers I know don't want crack or metamphetamine sold in Seven-Elevens – to quote one of the most pernicious accusations hurled by McCaffrey. What we're talking about is a new approach grounded not in fear, ignorance, prejudice and the vested pecuniary and institutional interests that drive current policies, but rather one grounded in common sense, science, public health and human rights.'

To Clinton, Barry McCaffrey must have seemed the perfect antidote to this headache. He was the youngest four-star general in the US Army and a former commander-in-chief of the US armed forces. And, with a massive $17.8 billion (£12.3 billion) federal drug control budget at his fingertips, he soon proved that his vehement anti-drugs pronouncements were not merely hot air. In 1998, less than two years into the job, 60,000 people were jailed for marijuana offences and a further 700,000 arrested for marijuana offences. McCaffrey was also keen to effect changes in the public's perception of the drug menace. Under his reign, around half of all American private companies introduced mandatory drug tests for their employees.

More controversially, he set up a covert arrangement with the TV networks in an effort to steer the nation's youth away from drugs. In exchange for a reduction in the number of mandatory public service announcements they must broadcast, McCaffrey's team were allowed to review scripts and see advance screenings of such popular teen programmes as *ER* and *Beverly Hills 90210* and suggest ways in which characters or plots could be changed to bolster the anti-drugs message.

When the lid was finally blown on the arrangement, there was understandable outrage in the Land of the Free. An editorial in the *New York Times* announced: 'In allowing government to shape or even be consulted on content in return for financial rewards, the networks are crossing a dangerous line they should not cross. On the far side of that line lies the possibility of censorship and state-sponsored propaganda.' Others claimed McCaffrey's arrangement was in direct contravention of the First Amendment, which guarantees the right to free speech.

Predictably, McCaffrey remained bullish in the face of his critics. 'It's been open, public and a wonderful thing because we're very proud that last year [1998] juvenile drug use declined by 13 per cent,' he said. Furthermore, he pointed to research that indicated, of the 168 prime time television episodes broadcast over three months in 1998, illegal drugs were seen being taken in only three per cent of the episodes, while tobacco was used in 19 per cent and alcohol in 71 per cent. 'These findings make it clear that the broadcast television industry is sending our kids the right messages about drug abuse,' McCaffrey said. He was backed by the networks themselves. 'We enjoy doing something that is socially responsible, especially since we reach a younger audience,' said Jamie Kellnee, chief executive of Warner Bros, while CBS denied that the independence or creative integrity of their programming had been compromised.

The storm was duly ridden. But, by the end of 2000, McCaffrey was beginning to realise that the writing was on the wall for him and his hard-line tactics. The Clinton administration was coming to an end, and the Bush campaign were strident in their claims that his war against drugs had failed, pointing out that while marijuana use among young Americans had declined, heroin and crack cocaine use had increased.

Moreover, the call for a radical rethink on drugs policy had expanded beyond the usual suspects that McCaffrey so despised. In June 2000, a number of respected judges from across the country went public in their calls for the restricted sale of cannabis, cocaine and heroin in order to break from what they saw as a vicious circle of violence and imprisonment. In a book entitled *Why Our Drugs Laws Have Failed and What We Can Do*

About It, more than 20 judges also suggested allowing individual states to decide on what drugs policy suited them best. Judge James P Gray, of Orange County, California, launched a scathing attack on McCaffrey himself. 'Asking him [McCaffrey] whether the right drugs policy is being pursued, is like asking a barber if one needs a haircut,' he said.

In October 2000, McCaffrey announced he intended to step down from his position. Like the equally tough Harry Anslinger 50 years before, he had made his mark against the drugs menace – but in winning a few battles he came no closer to winning the war. Mind you, McCaffrey would have been delighted to hear that his message had got through to at least some of the population. When 16-year-old Kerry Tucker discovered marijuana growing in the basement garden of her parents' house in Washington, she photographed the weed patch and took the prints down to the local police station.

> 'Marijuana has no therapeutic value, and its use is therefore always an abuse and a vice.' Harry J Anslinger, Commissioner of the US Bureau of Narcotics, 1953

Not only were her parents arrested, but her father lost his high-level job at the US Department of Energy and Kerry herself was ordered to stay with family friends and have no contact with her parents.

Barry McCaffrey's replacement, selected by President George W Bush, was former Republican Congressman Asa Hutchinson. But any hopes campaigners might have had that a new head of the DEA would herald new thinking about cannabis legislation – and especially medical use – appeared to be dashed in August 2001. Hutchinson made it clear that he intended to enforce the federal ban on medical marijuana, improve the accountability of paid confidential informants and increase the technology used in the war on drugs.

But spirits were raised somewhat in states like California and Oregon, which already allowed people to grow and dispense the drug on a strictly medicinal basis without fear of prosecution, when Hutchinson said: 'Currently, it's a violation of federal law. The question is how you address that from an enforcement standpoint. You're not going to tolerate a violation of the law, but at the same time there are a lot of different relationships...a lot of different aspects that we have to consider as we develop that enforcement policy.' They were also encouraged by the fact that, as Congressman, Hutchinson had supported local drug courts, which offer alternatives to prison.

The extent of Hutchinson's task – and McCaffrey's failure – was revealed when a survey monitoring drug use by teenagers placed cannabis as the drug of choice among juvenile offenders in the US. In the study, known as the Offender Urinalysis Screening program, marijuana was found in urine samples of 44 per cent of those tested at the state Department of Juvenile Justice facility in Baltimore. Overall, 43 per cent of teenagers tested positive for at least one drug, primarily marijuana. About one per cent tested positive for cocaine, opiates or amphetamine.

The study was based on more than 800 juveniles as they entered state detention centres between May 1999 and June 2000. Inmates told researchers that many of their peers see cannabis 'the same as cigarettes' and that it is easier to obtain than alcohol because you need an ID to purchase beer and liquor.

In the end, it was the Florida chads that sealed Al Gore's fate in the 2000 American Presidential election. But had Clinton's taciturn vice-president made it to the White House, however, it may well have been Lebanese Black that came back to haunt him. While Clinton famously did not inhale, Gore most certainly did – and on an industrial scale, according to a book entitled *Inventing Al Gore: A Biography* published in the run up to the election. Written by *Newsweek* correspondent Bill Turque, the book quotes John Warnecke, a friend of Gore's in the 1970s. 'We'd get stoned and talk about what we would do if we were President,' says Warnecke.

In 1987 Gore himself admitted 'infrequent and rare' cannabis consumption upon his return from the Vietnam war in 1971, but according to Turque: 'Warnecke and two other friends from Gore's Nashville days say Gore was an enthusiastic recreational user, smoking sometimes as often as three or four times a week; after hours at Warnecke's house, on weekends at the Gore farm or canoeing on the Caney Fork River.'

Not surprisingly, Gore and his former friend Warnecke have not spoken for 20 years.

'LEGALIZE IT!' – JAMAICA AND THE RASTAS

While the likes of the Beatles and the Rolling Stones took their cannabis lead from Bob Dylan, reggae star Bob Marley claimed to have an even more authoritative influence: God.

Genesis 1:12 says: '...and the earth brought forth grass, and herb yielding seed after his kind, and the tree yielding fruit, whose seed was in itself, after his kind: and God saw that it was good.' And Psalm 104:14 says: 'He causeth the grass to grow for the cattle, and herb for the service of Man...'

As a Rastafarian, Marley believed the instruction to smoke grass – or ganja as it is known in the Caribbean – came from none other than the Bible itself. And if you accept that by 'herb' the Bible is referring to cannabis and not chives, then Rasta logic is difficult to fault.

Rastafarians believe that Ras Tafari, Emperor Haile Selassie I of Ethiopia, who was crowned in 1930, is the living God. Their belief system originated in Jamaica in the 1920s. For believers, true salvation can only come to black people through repatriation to, or spiritual identification with, Africa. The smoking of ganja by Rastafarians is one aspect of the process by which they attempt to gain and develop insight into the central tenets of their beliefs. Bob Marley said that the smoking of ganja was to 'aid dere meditations on de truth'.

Cannabis had been taken to Jamaica by the East Indian labourers who replaced slave labour towards the end of the 19th century. The weed flourished and, happily for the locals, evolved into a particularly potent strain. Although the Rastafarians claim that they were influenced by biblical references, it has been pointed out that the use of ganja as a sacrament and aid to meditation is entirely logical in a country where it grows freely.

As the Rastafarian movement grew, the acceptance of use of 'the holy herb' grew with it. Since the 1960s its use has become an intrinsic part of Rastafarian culture and the religious reasons for its use unquestioned, although West Indian poet Linton Kwesi Johnson has his own, more mundane theory as to the drug's popularity in his homeland. He said: 'It [Rastafarianism] had a great deal which is positive in so far as it brought back to the masses a sense of dignity. It gave them a sense of pride in their

African heritage which British Colonialism has done a great deal to destroy. There are Rastas who...get high, and for a moment they can find themselves in Ethiopia at the foot of Selassie or sitting on the Golden Throne. But after the weed wears off...then it's back to the harsh and ugly reality of life.'

It may seem surprising that, despite its widespread use among the Rastafarian community, cannabis remains illegal in Jamaica. A main worry for the country's lawmakers is the risk of upsetting influential trade partners such as the USA by green-lighting free use of the drug. In the 1970s Jamaican politicians chose to ignore the findings of its own commission, which recommended no penalty for private use, a $10 (£6.90) fine for public use and that doctors should be able to prescribe marijuana. However, in October 1999, the Jamaican senate unanimously approved a resolution establishing another commission to explore the decriminalization of cannabis.

With the arrival of reggae music in the 1970s, cannabis culture had finally found its backing track. Reggae was predominantly the music of the Rastafarians, its laid back chugging rhythm a perfect accompaniment to the state of ganja intoxication that the Rastas believed essential to their beliefs. Its emergence as a global phenomenon is largely down to one man: Bob Marley.

Born in St Ann, Jamaica in 1945, the son of a white sailor and a black Jamaican teenager, Marley cut his teeth as a musician in local bars. And there he might have remained had he not, in 1967, been introduced to Rastafarianism. Marley embraced his new religion totally and, as a result, his own musical career was given a new impetus and direction. His songs of emancipation, spirituality and ganja enlightenment – the basic Rasta tenets – struck a chord not only in Jamaica but also around the world. Hits like 'I Shot The Sheriff', 'Stir It Up', 'Buffalo Soldier' and 'No Woman No Cry' made him an international star. And with albums entitled *African Herbsman* and *Kaya* (another name for ganja) he left people in no doubt about his influences. (Peter Tosh, a member of Marley's band The Wailers, was even more direct when he released an album called simply *Legalize It.*)

But Marley was keen for his message to be heard beyond the confines of the charts. He regarded himself as a Rasta prophet – and arch exponent of cannabis use. 'It's time to let the people get good herbs and smoke,' he

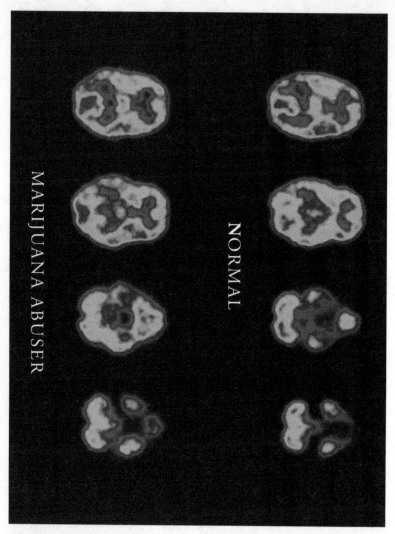

PET (Positron Emission Tomography) scans comparing the brain activity of a marijuana user (BOTTOM) with that of a non-marijuana user (TOP), with the front of the brain uppermost in the shot, showing progressively deeper slices from left to right. THC causes a lack of co-ordination, poor spatial judgement, and reduced brain activity in the cerebellum (LOWER RIGHT). In the normal brain, the cerebellum is an area of high activity.

George Washington (1732–99), first President of the USA. Cannabis – or, rather, hemp – was grown by the pioneers of the New World, including Washington and Thomas Jefferson. By the middle of the 19th century, as the commercial value of the plant fell, it became clear to the establishment that its use as a narcotic was rising. The east coast US cultural intelligentsia soon adopted the trends of the hashish houses of cosmopolitan Paris and London. Attendance at fashionable hash houses soon became *de rigueur* among the well-heeled, open-minded bright young things.

American actor Robert Mitchum (1917–97), shown here between takes during filming *The Angry Hills*, was arrested for marijuana possession in 1948 and served 60 days in prison. At the time, he thought he was ruined, but he later joked, 'It was the first vacation I've had in seven years, like Palm Springs without the riff-raff.'

Prince Ras Tafari (1891–1975), crowned Emperor Haile Selassie of Ethiopia in 1930, is regarded by Rastafarians as the living God. Followers of the faith, which originated in Jamaica in the 1920s, believe that true salvation can only come to black people through repatriation to, or spiritual identification with, Africa. The smoking of ganja by Rastafarians is one aspect of the process by which they attempt to gain and develop insight into the central tenets of their beliefs.

said in 1976. 'Government's a joke. All they want is ya to smoke cigarettes and cigars. Some cigars are wickeder than herb. Yeah, man – you can't smoke cigars. Smoke herb.'

By 1975, Marley was clearly a revolutionary standard bearer, the inheritor of the 1960s activist energy and hippie ganja enlightenment. Almost assassinated in 1976 in Kingston, Marley was given the United Nations Peace Medal on behalf of 500 million Africans in 1978 for his humanitarian achievements. He headlined a Peace Concert that same year in Jamaica, uniting the warring factions in the Kingston slums. But his greatest honour came when he was invited to headline the Zimbabwe Independence Celebrations in 1980. A year later Marley was dead, aged 36, of cancer.

In July 2001, British Prime Minister Tony Blair arrived on a flying visit to Jamaica. He was a determined man. Jamaica was in the middle of its commission into the possible legalization of its drugs laws, and Blair – having recently ruled out across-the-board legalization back home (see p79) – was determined to put a spanner in the works of the Jamaican effort. His main concern was the fact that 30 recent murders in Britain had been linked to Caribbean drugs gangs, better known as Yardies. His belief was that legalizing cannabis and other drugs in Jamaica would open up lucrative markets to the Yardies in the UK and lead to yet more gangland violence.

'We really have to strengthen not just our trade and investment, but policing and law enforcement so that we can tackle this evil trade that does so much damage here and in the UK and in the rest of the world,' he said.

DOPE CITY – AMSTERDAM AND THE 'DUTCH EXPERIMENT'

Amsterdam is *the* city of sex 'n' drugs 'n' *Van Der Valk*. To the oppressed cannabis smokers from other countries around the world, it may seem that to take a stroll down the Spuistraat, the Waterlooplein or the Nieumakt is akin to being a small child allowed free rein in a sweet shop. On every corner the tell-tale marijuana sign above a coffee house serves notice that here you can indulge in something exotic with your cappuccino. Inside, an aromatic fug assails the nostrils as you peruse the sort of menu you won't find in Betty's Tea Shop. Watch and learn as cannabis aficionados from all over the world sample the dozens of top-quality blends for sale. For just a few guilders you too can indulge in the delights of Black Hawaiian, Cytral Skunk, Thai, White Afghani or Kali Mist.

But even as you slip into a haze of dope-induced transcendence, there is one thing worth remembering. Cannabis, despite its abundance, its availability and its social setting, is actually illegal in the Netherlands. Marijuana has never been decriminalized in the Netherlands and outright legalization is a remote possibility. Instead, the Dutch authorities are the architects of a simple, but wholly unique approach to the drug: within reason, they turn a blind eye.

Up until 1976, however, it was a very different story. Drug offences were actively prosecuted and severely sanctioned, with such draconian punishment as 12 months imprisonment for minor cannabis offences being the norm. However, it soon became clear that despite the stiff sentences, cannabis use was rocketing, especially among Dutch youngsters. The pressure for reform began to bite during the cannabis-crazy 1960s – but whereas governments in the USA and the UK prevaricated and eventually introduced even stiffer penalties, in 1976 the enlightened Dutch acceded to popular demand and introduced the Opium Act.

The Act makes careful distinction between dangerous and less dangerous drugs. Penalties for trafficking heroin, cocaine and amphetamines are harsh and not open to debate. According to the Act, however, a number of activities are designated as 'not for prosecution, detection or arrest'. These include:

- the sale of less than 30g (1oz) of hemp products;
- dealing in, possessing or cultivating up to 5g (⅙oz) of marijuana.

And all the sales from coffee shops are taxed – an added bonus for the government.

As an experiment it was pioneering stuff. And so far the results have provided a slap in the face for those who argued that the country would end up staggering around in a pot-induced haze. Indeed, despite its availability, smoking pot remains a minority interest, with less than three per cent of Dutch people admitting to being regular tokers. As former Dutch drug tsar Eddy Engelsman observed, 'We succeeded in making pot boring.' And Bon Kreiser, head of drug care at the Dutch Health Ministry said: 'We do not believe in punishing young people for using cannabis for a short period of their life. We think it is irresponsible to give a young person a criminal record for something most will outgrow.'

However not everyone is convinced. There are claims that Holland is in the grip of a hard drugs frenzy directly related to the relaxed cannabis laws, with heroin addiction up 50 per cent, the highest rate of cocaine use among 14–16 year olds and increased use of amphetamines and drug-related crime. 'Our liberal drugs policy has been a failure, but its advocates are so rooted in their convictions that they cannot bring themselves to admit it,' says Dr Franz Kloopman, a leading drugs rehabilitation specialist in Holland.

Meanwhile recent United Nations figures estimate the global drugs trade to be worth a staggering $567 billion (£391 billion) annually – eight per cent of all global economic activity – and many European politicians see the Netherlands, and in particular Amsterdam, as an open gateway for drugs to pour into their own countries. It is a fact that, as far as many dealers are concerned, all roads lead to Amsterdam, and Liverpool's Curtis 'Cocky' Warren (see p132) is by no means the first or last foreign drug tycoon to take up temporary residence in tolerant Holland. In 1996 French President Jacques Chirac made Europe's unease clear when he threatened to scrap the Schengen Agreement, which allows unfettered movement across Europe's borders, amid charges that Holland had become a 'narco state'.

There are serious concerns within Holland itself. One complaint, especially among the country's conservatives, is that Holland's *laissez-faire* attitude to cannabis has created a booming drugs trade within its own borders. The Dutch marijuana industry is huge: some 35,000 farmers concentrate solely on producing potent, hydroponically grown cannabis crops of which two-thirds are sold through coffee shops. While that might be good economically, is it morally desirable?

Even the Dutch authorities responsible for the Opium Act are wary of creating a monster. They have sternly resisted calls for cannabis to be legalized fully because they fear losing the control they have now. Klaas Wilting, from the Amsterdam police force, said: 'Right now, legalization is not possible. We'd have a lot of problems. The Netherlands is a small country. I think you can only legalize when other countries want to do it too.'

Perhaps to pour oil on troubled Euro waters, the Dutch have been keen to display a degree of self-regulation. Recent amendments have included a reduction in the amount of cannabis that can be bought (5g/⅙oz) at a time rather than 30g/1oz) and the closure of dozens of coffee shops who have violated the rules.

'The coffee shops are strictly controlled by the police,' said Klaas Wilting. 'If there is a disturbance, or selling of hard drugs or stolen goods, we report this to the mayor and he closes the coffee shop.'

There have also been concerted efforts to clamp down on the main drugs gangs operating out of the major cities. And police also point out that they are keen to keep the lid on unauthorized shipments of cannabis from abroad. In 1995, the net haul of soft drugs comprised 44 per cent of the total intercepted within the 15-member European Union. At the same time, critics point out that this is an indication of the amount of cannabis filtering through the Netherlands.

FROM IGNORANCE TO BLISS – CANNABIS IN THE UK

Despite decades of protests from dedicated recreational users – which have included full-page adverts in *The Times*, mass rallies and blatant public smoking – cannabis is illegal in the UK. Indeed, until the recent decision to reclassify cannabis from a Class B to a Class C drug, British law clamped down harder on cannabis than any other western country.

The seeds of cannabis's doom were sown as long ago as 1798. This was the year the British East India Company foundered on a reef of debt, and the British government felt obliged to bale out the Empire's trading flagship. In a bid to recoup its substantial losses, the Crown decided to impose a tax on certain Indian industries, including those involved with the production and refinement of the widely used cannabis-based drugs bhang, ganja and charna. The government defended the punitive Indian Hemp Tax by arguing that it was good for the well-being of the colony: ganja, cheap and potent, was the preferred drug of the downtrodden masses and was blamed by the ruling colonists for the increasing outbursts of social unrest. The colonists were, in fact, all in favour of total prohibition. But the government realised that the natives were quite happy to pay over the odds for their ganja, which resulted in a substantial tax revenue for them.

As in France and the USA, more experimental use of the drug was left to those who frequented illicit hashish houses in London. Perhaps the most famous of these was the Rhymer's Club, which used hash in order to create a sense of the occult. Although not as grand as the Club de Hashishins in Paris, which boasted such luminaries as Beaudelaire and Gaultier among its members, Rhymers gained a reputation in Britain as being a place of ill-repute, with cannabis at the fore.

Throughout the 20th century, the British Home Office has always had a quaintly alarmist, if not faintly xenophobic, relationship with cannabis. Never sure how to deal with it, never fully convinced of its merits or deleterious effects, and always wary of its foreign origins, bureaucrats have time and again opted for the simple solution: keep it under lock and key in the furthest turret, and never mention its name at the dinner table.

The decision in 1911 by South Africa to ban cannabis – largely because of the effect it was having on its Indian diamond mine workers – led to a raft of international anti-drug legislation. The Hague Convention of 1912 led to the wholesale banning of opium, heroin and cocaine but, although cannabis was mentioned, it escaped regulation because opium was seen as the greatest threat at that time.

The roots of the drug's prohibition in the UK are suitably bizarre, and begin in 1922 when Home Office analysts were sent a strange substance that had been discovered in the coal shed of an Egyptian coffee house owner in South Shields on Tyneside. They soon identified the substance as 'hasheesh' – very odd, very suspicious, but not covered by the Dangerous Drugs Act of 1920. The following year, a ship bulging with 10 tonnes/tons of cannabis was detained in UK docks en route from Bombay to Djibouti. Again, the Home Office was consulted and again, after much chin-stroking, it was decided that as it was not covered by the Dangerous Drugs Act, there was little they could do. But by now, cannabis was beginning to pop up often enough to become irritating. Matters came to a head later that year when two waiters from Italy and Sudan were arrested in Soho, London and accused of offering to supply raw opium. In fact, the substance was the legal hashish, and the men were released. This provoked one irate Home Office official to sound off in the *Daily Mail*, and the resulting media-fuelled controversy led to the police recommending that cannabis be included in the Dangerous Drugs Act, advising that it had 'practically the same effect as cocaine and morphine upon its victims'.

> During 1997, the American Medical Association recommended controlled clinical trials on the medical uses of smoked marijuana, and the British Medical Association recommended trials of synthetic cannabinoids.

At the Home Office, pragmatism held sway. Officials noted that the result of cannabis prohibition in Egypt had merely been an increase in the price of the drug on the black market. To them, cannabis remained a mainly foreign curse that did not warrant legislation in this country. In the event, however, matters were taken out of their hands.

At the Geneva Conference on Opium in 1924-5, the Egyptians, overrun by hash, threw up their hands in despair and begged the League of Nations to bring in draconian international legislation to prevent its members from dealing or consuming the drug. To stress their point, the Egyptian delegate claimed cannabis was 'a dangerous narcotic, more harmful than opium,' and that 'about 70 per cent of insane people in lunatic asylums in Egypt are hashish eaters or smokers.'

The Egyptian pleas were enthusiastically embraced by the Americans, who were keen to enlist their help in their ongoing battle against opium and cocaine. From that moment, it was only a matter of months before the Geneva Conference ratified a ban on the import and export of Indian hemp except for certified medical or scientific purposes. The edict was met with great relief in the UK, where the Home Office immediately rescheduled cannabis as a poison and, in 1925, added it to a revised Dangerous Drugs Act. The Bill was passed by Parliament in doublequick time.

Very little changed over the next 30 years. In the 1950s, however, the authorities became aware that the definition of the drug was changing. The arrival of West Indian immigrants had led to a discernible increase in both use and interest in cannabis; and just as in New Orleans in the 1930s, it was the burgeoning jazz movement in London that raised the profile further. A series of raids in 1955 on jazz clubs netted only a handful of arrests, but served notice that the authorities were no longer prepared to turn a blind eye to cannabis use.

The advent of the 1960s, with flower-power influences from the USA and increasingly iconoclastic homegrown pop stars like The Beatles and The Rolling Stones, heralded the first major bust up between the pro-cannabis lobby and those who were against it. The Dangerous Drugs Act of 1964 created the new offence of cannabis cultivation. In 1966, folk singer Donovan was busted for possession fined £300 ($435) and warned ominously that 'it behoves you to behave yourself'. The arrest – and subsequent acquittal – of Mick Jagger and Keith Richards the following year proved that it would take more than the wagging finger of a magistrate to stop the growing tide of cannabis users in Britain.

The same year, 1967, a group called Soma – named after the narcotic in Aldous Huxley's *Brave New World* – published an open letter in *The Times* in which they denounced Britain's 40-year-old marijuana laws as 'immoral in principle and unworkable in practice'. The full-page letter was signed by more than 60 well known names including David Dimbleby, Jonathan Aitken and all four Beatles. A few weeks later, more than 3,000 people turned up at Hyde Park in London for a Soma-organized 'smoke-in'. Shortly afterwards, the government-commissioned Wootton Report, a review of the current drugs policies, concluded that possession of pot should be legalized. However, the government's response was the Dangerous Drugs Act of 1967, which introduced national powers to stop and search people and vehicles for drugs. And four years later, the 1971 Misuse of Drugs Act put the boot into cannabis even harder.

According to the Act, cannabis plants and resin became Class B drugs, on a par with amphetamines, some barbiturates and tranquillizers and even codeine. Cannabis oil, however, was a Class A drug, alongside heroin, cocaine, crack, LSD, ecstasy and any Class B or C drug that has been prepared for injection.

The maximum penalties under the Misuse of Drugs Act were draconian indeed – although the prospect of serving five years inside for having a tiny amount of Lebanese Black in your pocket was remote, unless it was part of a huge stash you were smuggling in from Amsterdam, of course.

Even before the reclassification of cannabis in October 2001, the law was seen as an ass both by users and police officers. Far from acting as a deterrent against cannabis use or distribution, more and more people were happy to risk the usual punishment of an appearance in magistrates' court. Why? Although the number of people dealt with for drugs offences involving cannabis rose from 40,194 in 1990 to 86,034 in 1997, less than 1,000 received custodial sentences.

According to one dealer, 'You get in front of the magistrate, you get a slap on the wrist and maybe a fine. It doesn't make any difference. You can get back the money you've had to cough up just by selling some more dope. I quite often end up selling gear to guys I've met in the waiting room in the court.'

Despite this derisory number of sentences, police forces across the country were obliged to devote much-needed manpower and hours to stop and searches. Over 300,000 were carried out for drugs in 1996-7 in England and Wales, bringing the total for four years to over a million. The swoop led to 134,500 arrests where drugs were found – the great majority of which were for cannabis.

Unrest was spreading, however. While the number of stop and searches had grown, the proportion where drugs had been found and arrests made had declined from 18 per cent in 1988 to 12 per cent in 1997/8. According to the Runciman Report of March 2000 (see pp77-9), stops and searches bore disproportionately on young people from minority ethnic communities in inner city areas.

The police were equally hacked off with what they increasingly saw as a waste of their precious resources. Sir John Stevens, Commissioner of the Metropolitan Police, said: 'Cannabis is a soft drug. If it were legalized we'd be fine with it because it's our job. Suppliers are still our emphasis.'

In 1969, a survey asked the British public whether cannabis should be legalized. One in eight agreed. In 1997, one in three agreed. With a new Labour government in power and a new mood of conciliation and debate surrounding the whole cannabis issue, it was clear that it was time for a new look at the cannabis situation in Britain.

'I'd be much more impressed if they criminalized alcohol and cigarettes,' says Fran Healy, lead singer of chart-topping band Travis. 'Nearly everybody in Britain smokes fucking hash, do you know what I mean? So whether or not it's legalized or not legal, you're just going to get a caution if you get done for it. It should be decriminalized but I'd rather people stop drinking. I hate drinking. Personally, I know someone who's a prosecutor for the state in Scotland and she says that all crime that they deal with – and they deal with a lot – at weekends and through the week, is drink-related. And never, ever, ever cannabis related. I think you're letting people get mad drunk and fighting and all that kind of stuff and there's loads and loads of things that are so stupid in law. But that's law. Law is stupid.'

Meanwhile Shaun Ryder, singer with The Happy Mondays, says: 'It's not harmful for you. It's good for you. If it does make you paranoid then you should stop smoking it. It doesn't make you go violent or crazy. You don't see anyone smoking three joints and then going and smashing someone's face in with a pint pot, do ya? That doesn't happen on marijuana. It's not a vicious drug. I don't know why it's illegal.'

These are, of course, viewpoints we might expect from members of the music industry, who have traditionally smoked cannabis on an industrial scale for years. But when it comes to decriminalization, Healy and Ryder have some influential and surprisingly 'establishment' backers. According to Peregrine Worsthorne, former editor of *The Sunday Telegraph*, criminalizing cannabis is 'a ridiculous thing to do – even more ridiculous than the American Prohibition idea, which, of course, was a terrible flop. You can't pass a law which a significant minority are not going to pay any attention to. You can't get crazier than that. I have smoked it. It wasn't for me. I'm an alcohol addict, so I didn't need anything extra. But so many friends do smoke it. It's now just a common occurrence.'

In 1998, the Police Foundation – the independent charitable research organization of which Prince Charles is a member – set up a committee to look at the drugs problem in Britain. Its brief was similar to that of the Wootton committee 30 years earlier. And, like the Wootton Report, when the Runciman Report was published in March 2000, its conclusions were political dynamite.

The committee was chaired by Dame Ruth Runciman, a 64-year-old veteran of campaigns and committees, and no stranger to controversy. A founding member of the Prison Reform Trust, which has campaigned for fewer criminals to be jailed and more lenient treatment of those who are imprisoned, Dame Runciman once said she had spent decades in public service on committees concerned with care of 'the sad, the mad and the bad.' In 1974, she was appointed by Labour Home Secretary Roy Jenkins to the Advisory Council on the Misuse of Drugs, serving until 1995. She also chaired an independent inquiry into the Misuse of Drugs Act in 1979, which recommended a relaxation in the laws on illegal substances.

The scope of the committee's investigations was vast, and included evidence from organizations as wide ranging as the Catholic Bishops Conference of England and Wales to the Cardiff Street Drugs Project. A number of surveys were commissioned into public attitudes towards drugs – and particularly cannabis. The committee also spent a week in Holland, talking to Dutch legislators and law-enforcers. For the most part, they were mightily impressed with what they observed. The committee concluded:

We think that the Dutch experience holds two important lessons for the United Kingdom. The first is the potential benefit from treating the possession and personal use of all drugs – not just cannabis – primarily as health problems. This should ensure that young people who experiment with drugs remain integrated into society rather than becoming marginalized. The second is the potential benefit from separating the market for cannabis from that of heroin. By doing so, the Dutch have provided persuasive evidence against the gateway theory of cannabis use, and in favour of the theory that if there is a gateway it is the illegal marketplace.

But the committee also noted:

> We recognize that, in the present political and cultural climate, it is difficult to see the introduction of Dutch-style coffee shops in the United Kingdom. The contradictions between domestic and international law and these practices are too great. The Dutch may be able to live with them, but they are likely to cause greater difficulties here. Nevertheless there may be developments that move us towards the Dutch experience, particularly as greater autonomy is devolved to local communities.

The committee's final conclusions on the cannabis question were unequivocal and scathing about the current state of the laws:

> The present law on cannabis produces more harm than it prevents... It inevitably bears more heavily on young people in the streets of inner cities, who are also more likely to be from ethnic minority communities.
>
> Cannabis is the drug most likely to bring people into contact with the criminal justice system. It is, by far, the drug most widely and commonly used. It is the drug most often involved in the main drug offences and is the drug that is most often seized. Because of the frequent use of discretion by the police and customs, it is the drug where there is the widest gap between the law as formulated and the law as practised.
>
> Cannabis is also less harmful than the other main illicit drugs, and understood by the public to be so. If our drugs legislation is to be credible, effective and able to support a realistic programme of prevention and education, it has to strike the right balance between cannabis and other drugs.

The report's main recommendations were that cannabis should be transferred from Class B to Class C, and that possession for personal use should no longer be an imprisonable offence.

The 148-page report took two years to compile and concluded that implementation of their recommendations would 'bring the law into line with public opinion and its most loyal ally, common sense'. However, it took the Labour government just a few short hours to summarily dismiss its findings. A government statement said: 'We don't support the recommendations for a reclassification. The Prime Minister believes that whilst it is right that the greatest harm is done by hard drugs, it would send out the worst possible signal if we were to soften our laws in the way being suggested.'

If the Runciman Report was rubbished by the government, its immediate legacy was a major public debate about the pros and cons of legalizing cannabis for recreational and medical use, and a furious backlash from users sick of having their arguments summarily thrown back in their faces.

Arguments raged in the Press as advocates from both sides took up their cudgels. Indeed the debate at times assumed an almost surreal edge as traditionally left-wing and liberal newspapers like *The Guardian* and *The Independent* were joined by staunch right-wing publications *The Times*, the *Sunday Telegraph* and even the arch-conservative *Daily Mail* in calling for a sensible debate over the matter. Although they avoided calling for an all-out decriminalization of recreational cannabis, even the most fervent of right-wing commentators were in favour of it for medical use. And all were infuriated by the government's intransigence and refusal to even entertain a debate.

'Those who have argued for decriminalization in the past have been dopeheads,' said the *Daily Telegraph* editor Charles Moore. 'We don't think drugs are a good thing but we want a debate.'

Suddenly, policy makers were being asked awkward questions – especially those who were bright young things in the Swinging '60s. Asked on a television debate whether she had ever tried cannabis, former Northern Ireland Secretary Mo Mowlam said she had, that she had inhaled and that she hadn't enjoyed it. Meanwhile maverick Labour backbencher Clare Short observed that, 'If the Press asked every member of the Cabinet if they had ever tried cannabis, most of them would have to lie.'

Despite the jokes, there was a serious underlying message, which was outlined by Mike Linnell, of the addicts support group Manchester Lifeline: 'People's and the government's attitudes have changed because of experience,' he said. 'There aren't many people who haven't been affected by drugs in some way. Even Cabinet ministers have admitted trying drugs in their youth. Everyone, it seems, does it.'

Linnell was one of a number of drug counsellors who were delighted that the debate was now out in the open and that their serious message could be put across. Danny Kushlik, of the pressure group Transform, said: 'Drugs need to be legalized because they're dangerous, not because they're safe. The way to control and regulate drugs is by bringing them back into the economy and not pushing them underground.'

One of the more controversial comments came from Sir John Stevens, commissioner of the Metropolitan Police and Britain's leading policeman. He said: 'Smoking cannabis is not a priority because we have to concentrate on the upsurge in robberies and murders in London. If you go to the Tube in London and don't pay, that also is not a priority for the police, but if we catch someone doing it then we have to enforce the law. Arresting people for cannabis is low on my list of priorities.'

Opponents of cannabis were caught somewhat flat-footed in the face of such establishment revisionism, but they soon fought back. Home Office minister Charles Clarke – who himself admitted smoking marijuana as a student – laid down the government line, indicating that there were no plans to de-penalize possession of cannabis: 'I believe the most likely impact of a relaxation in the law would be to increase consumption of those drugs. I think that would be bad for the people concerned and bad for society.'

Janet Betts, whose daughter Leah died after taking ecstasy, said: 'We already have decriminalized drugs. If a person found with drugs can convince a police officer they are for their own use, they get nothing more than an instant caution. If cannabis is decriminalized, what is next? Ecstasy?'

> The DEA has grown into a second international intelligence agency, with a global network of agents rivalling that of the CIA.

Meanwhile Paul Stoker, director of the National Drugs Prevention Alliance pointed out: 'The fact that more people who use cannabis go on to abuse hard drugs is beyond argument. There are now more reasons than ever to keep cannabis illegal.'

The British Medical Association trundled out its usual line on the risks of cannabis smoking: 'Smoking a cannabis cigarette leads to three times greater tar inhalation than smoking a cigarette. Chronic cannabis smoking increases the risk of cardiovascular diseases, bronchitis, emphysema and probably lung cancer.'

But it was left to the then Home Secretary Jack Straw to put the final word on the debate:

Cannabis is a controlled drug for good scientific reasons. Both the World Health Organization and our own BMA have repeatedly concluded that cannabis is harmful. Were cannabis legalized, it is highly probable that consumption would rise. The price would fall as the premium in the price today for the criminal risk which dealers carry fell away and as dealers piled into the UK from across Europe. The more government tried to choke off demand by taxing cannabis, the greater the incentive for criminals to engage in smuggling. There are many, of course, who are prepared to break the law at present to take cannabis, but the fact that it is illegal does limit its use. I accept that making cannabis legal would not necessarily greatly increase addiction to hard drugs... But what would almost certainly happen is that the UK would take over from the Netherlands as the European drug trade.

Despite the fact her report had been put on the back burner indefinitely by the government, Lady Ruth Runciman remained defiant. 'My report will have a longer shelf-life than this government,' she said.

Ironically, it was to be a leading member of the main opposition party whose ill-judged opinions of cannabis law were to give the most startling indication of how opinions had changed...

When Shadow Home Secretary Ann Widdecombe stood up to address the Conservative Party at their annual conference in October 2000, she had a bombshell to deliver:

Today I am able to announce a new policy. Earlier this year I visited New York, where under Mayor Giuliani crime has plummeted. Although we can't replicate exactly what I saw there, we can learn the lessons of tackling crime head on and not conceding a centimetre to the criminals. So today, I can announce a new policy. A policy that means no quarter for those whose trade is dealing in human misery, despair and even death. And so, from, the possession of the most minimal amount of soft drugs right up the chain to the large importer, there will be no hiding place. There will be zero tolerance.

Parents want it. Schools need it. Our future demands it. The next Conservative government will do it. What does it mean? It means zero tolerance of possession. No more getting away with just a caution, no more hoping that a blind eye will be turned. If someone possesses drugs, the minimum for a first offence will be £100 ($145). But not for a second offence. Then it's into court.

Almost immediately after her speech, critics were lining up to take a pop at Widdecombe. Leading the way was the Police Superintendents' Association, who pointed out that the manpower and resources needed to lock up every person they found in possession of the smallest amount of cannabis would be astronomical. Not only that, but a hard-line approach to drugs would do much to destroy the fragile co-existence the police force had been trying to build up with an increasingly cynical public.

'My view of Ann Widdecombe's proposal is that it is impractical to an extent which proves that the Tory party is totally out of touch with 21st-century Britain,' said Labour peer Roy Hattersley.

Meanwhile, journalist Andrew Neil said: 'I've never tried it because I'm a rebel and in the '60s everybody was taking it. I didn't like the smell so I'm not happy to be in a room where everybody's smoking it. But if I'm walking down the King's Road and a bunch of kids are coming the other way I'd rather they were high on a bit of weed than tanked up on Carlsberg. I think [Ann Widdecombe's proposal] is bonkers. When you think of all the problems of crime, to start picking up kids because they've got a couple of pieces of marijuana is bizarre.'

'They have got completely the wrong end of the stick,' Widdecombe explained hurriedly. 'They thought they would have to do it on present resources, and secondly they thought it would remove all discretion.'

Even as she spoke, however, the Shadow Home Secretary was reeling under a second onslaught – this time from members of her own party. The weekend after the conference, one Sunday newspaper revealed that no less than seven of Widdecombe's Shadow Cabinet colleagues – including Shadow Home Secretary Francis Maude – had cheerfully admitted smoking cannabis in their youth. Meanwhile Peter Ainsworth, the Shadow Culture Secretary, dismissed her policy as 'unrealistic', former Prime Minister John Major called for a rethink and Conservative vice-chairman Steve Norris said it was a tall order to expect the police to impose zero tolerance against a backdrop of falling police numbers. More importantly, as far as the Party were concerned, Norris realized that Widdecombe's comments were as far removed from the opinions of the crucial youth vote as it was possible to be.

Seeing her grand scheme disintegrating before her eyes, Widdecombe made a desperate attempt to salvage some face. 'The use of the phrase zero tolerance in this area was unfortunate because everybody has their own interpretation of what zero tolerance is,' she said. 'I should have made it clear that zero tolerance does not mean you come down on every single instance of possession. It means you challenge every instance, but the police have got to have the right to decide whether they do go forward. I was trying to ensure that where they did want to go forward, they have more teeth than now.'

Sadly for Ann Widdecombe, it was left to Liberal Democrat leader Charles Kennedy to sum up the true impact of her speech. 'She has performed a public service in the past few days by showing how far public attitudes have changed.'

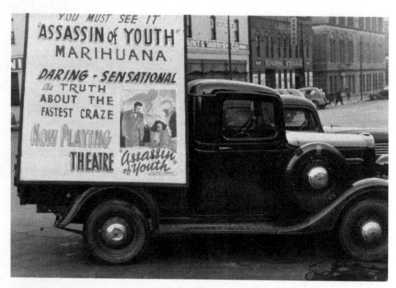

A truck in Omaha, Nebraska, carrying a poster advertising 'Assassin of Youth'. Harry J Anslinger, the ambitious head of the Federal Bureau of Narcotics, was fanatical in his attack on what he saw as a cancerous cannabis sub-culture eating away at the heart of America. But rather than clamp down with police raids, as he had done during Prohibition, he issued a series of scabrous anti-cannabis articles in magazines and newspapers. *Marihuana: Assassin Of Youth* (1937) was without doubt the best known diatribe.

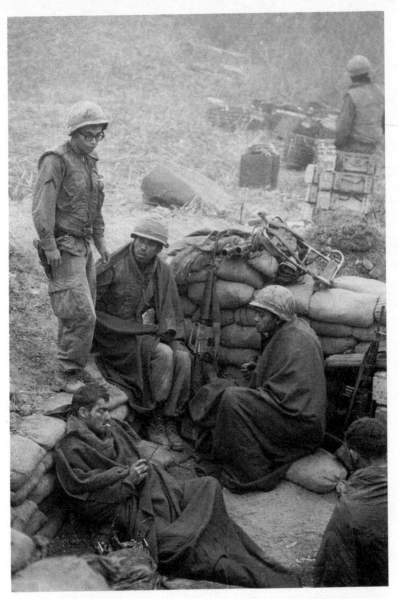

US soldiers in a dug-out on Hill Timothy in Vietnam, April 1968. The conflict in Vietnam is remembered largely as a war fought under the influence of drugs: 75 per cent of the draft who went to Vietnam lived through the daily horrors they faced by smoking marijuana. To the chagrin of the US Army's generals, the battlefields were a source of cheap and plentiful grass. Many of those who returned alive introduced it to other young people and its use quickly became widespread. By the late 1960s, a whole counter-culture had emerged whose desire was to drop out of society, and their drug of choice was cannabis. The hippie movement had begun.

A POWERLESS DRUGS TSAR AND A REVOLUTIONARY HOME SECRETARY

We have already encountered ass-kicking General Barry McCaffrey, the man charged by Bill Clinton with ridding the United States of the drugs menace. Following Clinton's lead, in 1998 Tony Blair appointed a drugs tsar of his own in the shape Keith Hellawell, former Chief Constable of both Cleveland and West Yorkshire forces. In many ways, Hellawell was the complete antithesis of McCaffrey: a thoughtful, self-effacing man who believed fervently that the drugs issue was not one that was simply black and white. Two different tsars, two different cultures, two different approaches. Yet by 2001, both had been perceived as having failed dismally in the battle against drugs, and both were looking for new jobs.

When Keith Hellawell took over as drugs tsar, he arrived full of bright and innovative ideas about dealing with the problem. There was no question of a knee-jerk reaction, no suggestion of hard line clamping down. Instead, Hellawell took to the job many of the philosophies of treatment and re-education that had made him such a popular and respected Chief Constable on the streets of Middlesbrough and Bradford. 'In Bradford, back during the riots, when I was Chief Constable there, we reduced burglary in one year by 62 per cent in a very sensitive area by targeting prolific criminals and picking up the root cause of why they were doing that,' he said, shortly after taking over the job. 'Some people are bad people, but a lot of people are driven to it by all sorts of reasons.'

As drugs tsar, Hellawell believed in drug workers active in every police station and in every school, and listening to those involved in the drug world – especially addicts. And, initially, the results were encouraging. After a year in the job, Hellawell's methods were attracting the attention of experts from around the world who were fascinated by this cutting edge approach to the drug conundrum.

One of Hellawell's innovations was the appointment of an anti-drugs chief to every council in the country, a move that was designed to dispense with campaigns run by police, health and educational authorities and other agencies.

But things started to go wrong for Hellawell just as the public perception on cannabis began to change. Those who imagined him as a breath of fresh air in the debate about specific legalization (he had advocated it when Chief Constable) were sorely disappointed when he sided firmly with the government over the rejection of the Runciman Report. They were also dismayed when he failed to stand by his nominal boss, Mo Mowlam, who argued for a clearer demarcation between hard and soft drugs.

But most of all they could not believe that a policeman who had identified and improved social problems in areas like Bradford, could not seem to grasp the damning statistic that although Britain's anti-drugs laws were the harshest in Europe, its population still consumed the most hard and soft drugs.

When David Blunkett took over from Jack Straw in the Home Office in May 2001, Hellawell's days were numbered. But by then, his stock had already been tarnished in too many people's eyes.

'He became lapdog of a government that has insisted on maintaining a hard-line stance on drugs,' said The Guardian newspaper in a damning leader. 'He lined up with Ministers in rejecting the idea of reclassifying drugs according to their harm and paid far too little attention to the wide variation between police forces on their cautioning policies.

By the time David Blunkett sidelined him, he was a sad and peripheral Whitehall figure. He leaves a strategy which still places far too much emphasis on police and customs and far too little on treatment and education.'

But although he had been dumped by the government, Hellawell remained a part of the drugs debate. He was given a two-day a week role as a part-time adviser on international drug issues, which included helping countries who had applied for membership of the European Union to develop anti-drugs strategies.

The appointment of David Blunkett to the job of Home Secretary had an immediate effect on Britain's cannabis laws. Blunkett, it appeared, not only agreed with the thrust of the Runciman Report, but was prepared to act upon it, and quickly. His first move was to take over control of drugs policy from Mo Mowlam. He then began to exercize a series of measures that would have been inconceivable a few short weeks earlier. In July 2001, just two months into the job, Blunkett gave his tacit go-ahead to police in Brixton, South London, who wanted to abandon prosecuting people caught with cannabis. Instead, they would be given a 'stiff telling off', and their stash confiscated. In effect, it was the equivalent of the old-fashioned clip round the ear from the local bobby. According to the area commander, Brian Paddick, there was little point in two officers spending hours charging a suspect only for them to be fined £25 ($36) in the magistrates court.

The Brixton experiment was initially a six-month trial only, and applied to people found with only small amounts of the drug in their possession – but to the legalization lobby, it was a ray of sweet sunshine.

Sir David Ramsbotham, the outgoing chief inspector of prisons, said: 'The more I think about it and the more I look at what's happening, the more I can see the logic of legalizing drugs, because the misery that is caused by the people who are making a criminal profit is so appalling, and the sums are so great that are being made illegally that I think there is merit in legalizing and prescribing, or whatever, so people don't have to go and find an illegal way of doing it.'

In the face of such pro-legalization glee, Blunkett suddenly appeared to turn cagey. A week after the start of the Brixton experiment, he made it clear that he was not opening the door to legalization and insisted there was 'no easy way forward'. He also opposed a Royal Commission on the legalization of drugs, proposed by the Liberal Democrats. But, clearly not wanting to be regarded as another big talking, no-action politician, he did something that no other Home Secretary had done regarding the cannabis issue: he hedged his bets. 'There is room for an adult, intelligent debate,' Blunkett said, 'but it isn't "are you for or against?" It's "let's think, let's consider, let's not be pushed by articles in newspapers or hysteria."'

The total spent on the War on Drugs rose from $537 million (£370 million) in 1980 to $1.2 billion (£828 million) in 1984. By 1991, the US government was spending $7.7 billion (5.3 billion) on action against illegal intoxicants.

In Brixton, meanwhile, the radical policy was credited with freeing up hundreds of hours of police time and allowing them to concentrate on more serious crime – but many residents claimed it gave the dealers a new-found confidence and made even hard drugs more widely available than before. Many dealers were soon boasting of having received three or four separate warnings since the new scheme began. One shopkeeper said: 'In the last few months, all the dealers have become more confident. They think they're untouchable.'

The biggest cannabis dealers say they shift a kilo (2¼lb) a week, netting them around £800 ($1,180) in profit. Most of the customers are from outside the area, largely middle-class whites. They are drawn to the area knowing that even if they are caught buying, they won't end up with a criminal record. An internal review conducted by senior officers at Scotland Yard concluded that over the first six months of the scheme, 1,400 man hours were freed up. The number of seizures of cannabis rose by a third while seizures of Class A drugs rose by 19 per cent.

In the six months before the scheme, 278 arrests for possession were made. In the six months that followed, more than 400 warnings for possession were issued. For many, this is proof that the area is now a magnet for drug buyers across London.

There was still a chink of light but the door had, to all intents and purposes, been shut again. It would not remain that way for long.

What with the Brixton experiment and Blunkett's debate, one of the more extraordinary developments in the serpentine history of cannabis and the UK law went largely unnoticed. A shadowy organization consisting of the heads of MI6, MI5, the Customs and Excise investigation branch, the National Criminal Intelligence Service, the police National Crime Squad and the Association of Chief Police Officers, not to mention the permanent under-secretaries of the Home Office, Foreign Office and Ministry of Defence had all been discussing Britain's on-going battle with drug smugglers. The conclusions of the Cabinet Office Committee, Concerted Inter-Agency Drugs Action (CIDA) amounted to the most radical shift in drugs policy for a generation. Under the new strategy, Britain was to abandon the hunt for cannabis smugglers and dealers. Instead, large-scale cannabis seizures and prosecutions would only take place as a by-product of investigations into Class A drugs like cocaine and heroin.

'It's not that we plan to stop seizing cannabis when we come across it,' one senior Customs source said. 'However, the need to focus on Class

A drugs means cannabis seizures will now take place as a by-product, not as an end to themselves.'

What the source was referring to was the government's avowed drugs target of reducing Class A consumption by half by 2008. With shock statistics revealing that Britons were now consuming up to 36,000kg (80,000lb) of heroin and 41,000kg (90,000lb) of cocaine – twice as much as previous official estimates for the whole of western Europe – cannabis users had suddenly paled into insignificance.

On 23 October 2001, Home Secretary David Blunkett finally did what UK pro-cannabis campaigners had clamoured for, but never dared believe would ever happen. On that day Blunkett announced that the UK's laws covering cannabis were to be eased so possession would no longer be an arrestable offence. Although the drug would remain illegal under Blunkett's proposals, it would be re-classified from a Class B to a Class C drug – alongside mild amphetamines, tranquillizers such as temazepam and Valium and anabolic steroids. He said that the aim was to free police to concentrate on harder drugs and improve current legislation so it will 'make more sense' to people on the street.

But he was careful not to suggest this was a complete relaxation of cannabis laws. Possession and supply would remain a criminal offence, attracting maximum sentences of five years for supply and two for possession. But he hinted that police, rather than arresting people caught with cannabis, would be more likely to issue a warning, a caution or a court summons.

Meanwhile, Blunkett announced that the licensing of cannabis derivatives for medical use – such as the relief of multiple sclerosis symptoms – would be given government backing if trials proved to be successful. 'We believe it is right to look at the re-categorization of cannabis,' the Home Secretary told a House of Commons Home Affairs Select Committee. 'I shall therefore be putting to the Advisory Council on the Misuse of Drugs a proposal that we should re-categorize cannabis to 'C' rather than 'B', thereby allowing police to concentrate their resources on class 'A' drugs – crack cocaine and heroin in particular – and to ensure that whilst they are able to deal with those pushing and dealing in drugs in exactly the same way as they can at the moment, it will both lighten their load and make more sense on the streets than it does at the moment.'

The reclassification of cannabis was seen as the greatest decision ever taken by a Home Secretary, or as the worst, depending on your viewpoint. Within hours of Blunkett's announcement, proponents from both sides of the argument were clashing heads in a battle that promises to rage on and on for years to come.

Veteran journalist and pro-cannabis activist Rosie Boycott described it as: '...a significant day for those who believe in personal freedom – and for those who believe in a stable and honest society in which the law of the land is respected, and not treated with casual disregard. I belong in both camps, which is why I have long campaigned for the complete legalization of cannabis. David Blunkett's intention to downgrade this harmless substance from a Class B drug to a Class C drug is a welcome first step on the road to sanity. Even so, the Home Secretary is far from being revolutionary. He is too cautious for my taste.'

One of Boycott's – and Blunkett's – critics was Susan Greenfield, professor of pharmacology at Oxford University. In her view, the decision was the beginning of the rocky road to ruin. 'I fear that this move could have disturbing consequences for our society,' she said, 'particularly on young people who will now be given the message that they need not worry about substance misuse.

My concern goes even further. It is said, through decriminalization, we will encourage the development of a society where millions of young people are demotivated, thinking about only their next fix instead of looking at broader horizons, regarding drugs as the solution to all their problems. A world where, in the words of the Dutch Health Ministry, we have a generation who "crawl out of bed in the morning, go grab a joint, smoke another joint and don't know what to do with their lives". We should heed those words before going any further.'

Greenfield's words were backed up by a report that came out around the same time in which England and Wales were dubbed the drug 'capitals' of the European Union, with more cannabis users than any other member state. In the survey, nearly 1 in 10 adults admitted having taken cannabis within the previous 12 months, the highest in the EU. Britain also had the largest number of young users, with two in five 15- and 16-year-olds saying they have experimented. The EU drugs agency in Lisbon, which carried out the survey, said cannabis was the widest available and most commonly used drug in the EU and that only Denmark rivalled Britain for cannabis use. Over the previous 12 months, 9 per cent of British adults and 23 per cent of 16- to 29-year-olds said they had used cannabis while in Denmark the figures were 3.3 and six per cent respectively. Spain had the second highest usage, 7.6 per cent of adults, followed by 5.2 in Holland, 4.7 in France, 4.5 in Germany, 4.4 in Greece, 1.9 in Finland and 1.5 in Belgium and 1 per cent in Sweden. Curiosity was the usual motive for the younger age group trying the drug, said the drugs agency.

SAME OLD STORY – CANNABIS LAWS IN THE REST OF THE WORLD
AUSTRALIA
Penalties for cannabis offences vary from state to state. Since the '70s several states have lessened penalties for possession, cultivation and use of small amounts of cannabis. In 1987 South Australia, followed in 1992 by the Australian Capital Territories, introduced expiation notice schemes, which required on-the-spot fines for minor cannabis offences; if the fine is paid promptly, no court appearance or criminal record is necessary but, if not, a court appearance will follow. Recently, the Northern Territory, Victoria and West Australia have followed suit and introduced cautioning. The trend at reducing penalties for possession has been matched by harder penalties for supply.

AUSTRIA
Use is a criminal offence, resulting in a fine or custodial sentence.

BELGIUM
On 21 April 1998 Belgium officially decriminalized cannabis, which means, in practice, that those caught in possession for personal consumption will not be prosecuted but industrial production and dealing will not be tolerated.

In 2001, it announced that, under radical plans approved by the cabinet, it will soon be legal to grow, import and consume potentially unlimited amounts of pot for personal use in Belgium. 'Any possession of cannabis for personal consumption will no longer provoke a reaction from the justice system unless its use is considered to be problematic or creates a social nuisance,' the Health Minister, Magda Aelvoet, said. Legislation is due to be passed by the end of 2002.

CANADA
In 2001, Canada became the first country to legalize cannabis for medical use. This effectively undoes its 1961 Federal Narcotic Control Act, which made it illegal to possess, traffic, possess for trafficking, cultivate, import or export cannabis.

CUBA
In February 1999, the Cuban Parliament approved a law that introduced the death penalty for the possession, production, and trafficking of drugs.

CZECH REPUBLIC
In January 1999, despite the efforts of former President and 1960s hippie Vaclev Havel, the Czech government made 'more than a small amount' of marijuana illegal. Before this law was drafted, marijuana was technically legal for personal consumption.

DENMARK
Cannabis is allowed to be grown, sold and consumed in an area that is part of Copenhagen. Unfortunately, the people who live there are mostly poor and the area is quite run down, which gives cannabis a bad image in the press.

EGYPT
In 1868, possession was made a capital offence. In 1874, importation was allowed but not possession. Then in 1879 importation was again made illegal and in 1884 growing also became a criminal offence. These laws

were reissued in 1891 and 1894. It is still illegal today, although many locals smoke. Crops in the Sinai are being destroyed and westerners are being given long sentences by the courts.

FINLAND
Use remains a criminal offence.

FRANCE
According to Article 630 of the French public health regulations, French citizens are banned from 'portraying in a favourable light and promoting or inciting the consumption of any product classed as a banned substance.' And, in April 2001, French prosecutors proved that the authorities mean business when they demanded 12-month prison terms for two activists who were caught wearing T-shirts with a picture of a cannabis leaf on them. The accused – Jean-Pierre Galland, president of the Cannabis Information and Research Collective, and Laurence Duffy, head of the campaign group's Lyon branch – were also brought to book for selling CDs entitled *Eine Kleine Hemp Musik.*

The case brought into the open a growing division between those who believe in enforcing Article 630 to the letter, and those who believe the French authorities' attitude towards cannabis is not only ludicrously heavy-handed, but also wildly out of sync with what the majority of the country thinks.

In theory, the possession and selling of cannabis is banned and anyone caught importing just a few grams can be jailed for up to 30 years. Yet figures indicate that some 7 million of the country's 60 million population have tried the drug at least once, while 2 million are regular users. Even members of the former Socialist French government came clean about their use of cannabis in the past. Dominique Voynet, the Green's environment minister, caused a minor scandal when she admitted toking on the occasional joint and called for decriminalization. 'I am more worried by the number of French people who need sleeping pills than by the number of people who confess to having smoked a joint,' she said. Lionel Jospin, who was then leader of the former Socialist government, also admitted smoking cannabis in his youth.

In many ways, the French situation mirrors that of the UK's. While the conservative opposition, headed by President Chirac, were firmly against any relaxation in the laws, the former Socialist government under Jospin came under increasing pressure from both within and without to address the problem. In 2000, France's inter-ministerial drugs commission recommended a softer approach, while the justice minister wrote to every judge in the country urging them to avoid prison sentences for offences relating to personal cannabis consumption.

Meanwhile, the trumped-up charges against Jean-Pierre Galland and Laurence Duffy served only to focus the ire of the pro-cannabis lobby. In an open letter to Mr Jospin, over 40 prominent people, including philosophers, Green MPs, actors, singers and leading human rights activists, claimed that it was absurd that 'in France, the birthplace of human rights, in the year 2001, you can no longer be jailed for consuming cannabis but you can for "portraying its consumption in a favourable light".'

Galland remained defiant, despite the threat of jail . In a letter to over 570 Members of Parliament, he included a rolled spliff and the words: 'Nurtured and cosseted by enthusiasts, this cannabis, raised under the sweet skies of France, has been generously donated by growers to give to you. A law that is broken daily by hundreds of thousands of people is a bad law. It is time for the state to stop treating cannabis enthusiasts like delinquents.'

GERMANY

Germany's narcotic laws prohibit the importing, exporting and processing of cannabis, although cultivation of cannabis as a beet-breeding agent is allowed provided the plants do not flower. Smoking a joint is illegal, but a landmark ruling from Germany's constitutional court in 1994 means possession of small amounts for personal use is not usually prosecuted.

GREECE

The Greek authorities have stopped prosecuting those in possession of small amounts of cannabis. In 1999 stiff prison sentences for possessing recreational drugs such as marijuana were revoked, although smokers caught red-handed are still required to have long periods of counselling.

The state has also funded the opening of 36 therapeutic and drug prevention centres in less than a year.

GREENLAND
In remote Greenland the authorities are fighting a losing battle against what is a thriving trade in the weed. 'The drug is illegal, but it is impossible to fight the massive cannabis trade in Greenland as it involves the whole of society' said Hans Haahr, chief of Greenland's Drug Squad.

The Drug Squad estimates that the trade in cannabis is worth US$75 million (£52 million), which is equivalent to nearly 10 per cent of the annual gross national product, including the economic assistance from Denmark. This makes the cannabis trade Greenland's third largest industry measured in annual turnover.

Businessmen are involved, according to the police, as they accept drug money and launder it in trading with snowscooters, boats and stereo equipment. Large segments of the population smoke cannabis regularly, while businesses earn millions through money laundering. All social groups smoke cannabis and there are also school teachers who sell cannabis to pupils.

INDIA
Confusion and corruption surrounding the drugs laws abound in India – but the safest policy is not to be caught smoking cannabis. The Indian government has clamped down, making little distinction between soft and hard drugs. Anyone charged with illegal possession risks a mandatory ten-year jail sentence and, under Indian law, you are guilty until proved innocent. In 1997, the *Footprint Guidebook to Goa* warned that in 18 months since November 1995, 21 foreigners were imprisoned for drug offences. The local police deny that bribery is rife, but many more foreigners who have been caught smoking joints admit they have bought their way out of trouble.

IRELAND
Use is a criminal offence, but first and second-time offenders are only fined. Thereafter custodial sentences can be awarded.

ITALY

Since April 1998 possession of drugs for personal consumption and small-scale cultivation of cannabis are no longer criminal offences. This move followed a 1992 referendum in which 52 per cent were in favour of decriminalizing possession of cannabis. Possession is now subject to administrative sanctions rather than criminal prosecution, but cultivation, sale and delivery remain illegal. Loopholes in the present law allow personal use but not personal cultivation.

LUXEMBOURG

In May 2001, a groundbreaking bill decriminalized cannabis, making its personal use and possession a civil, as opposed to criminal, offence and therefore subject only to fines.

JAPAN

Cannabis was made illegal in Japan by the post-World War II occupying US administration in 1948 – even though it grows abundantly in the wild. Every year in Japan over a million wild cannabis plants are destroyed by narcotics agents. Possession of cannabis can bring prison sentences of up to five years and cultivating or trading in cannabis can bring prison sentences of up to seven years.

MALAYSIA

Definitely *not* the place to be caught with an eighth in your back pocket. Malaysia's drug laws prescribe the mandatory death penalty for people trafficking in more than 15g (½oz) of heroin or 200g (7oz) of cannabis. More than 100 people, around a third of them foreigners, have been hanged in Malaysia for drug offences since the mandatory death sentence for trafficking was introduced two decades ago.

MOROCCO

African and Asian countries may give the appearance that cannabis is legal already but it remains illegal and many foreigners have to buy their way out of trouble. However, many of the locals smoke it themselves –

especially kif, a mixture of leaf cannabis and black (illegal) tobacco. In the Katama area, in the North in the mountains, huge crops of cannabis are grown, providing valuable income through sales to the rest of the world. Possession is not prosecuted in Katama. Elsewhere in Morocco it is usually possible to bribe your way out of a court appearance, which is why police often arrest foreigners.

NEW ZEALAND

In March 1999, the New Zealand government ruled out the legalization of cannabis. Indeed it went so far as to propose a ban on paraphernalia such as pipes or bongs, with a maximum three-month jail sentence and £1,000 (US$1,500) fine for anyone caught in possession. However east of Auckland, on the rugged Coromandel peninsular, a quiet rebellion is under way. It was here in recent elections that the rest of New Zealand was shocked when seven Green Party MPs were returned to Parliament. By far the most controversial was Nandor Tanczos, a young dreadlock-sporting, dope-smoking Rastafarian. Tanczos and his Green colleagues are dead set on reforming the drug laws and, more specifically, on legalizing cannabis – and they have the support of many young people. According to recent research, more than half of New Zealand's population between the ages of 15 and 45 admit to having used pot, which is the highest per-capita rate in the world.

The country has a ready supply of cannabis. Deep in the forests of Northland, near the Bay of Plenty, are plantations that supply the Auckland markets. The plantations are run predominantly by Maoris, who claim that because they have no work they have no alternative but to grow pot. A recent report, by Auckland University's geography department, estimated that the street value of cannabis seized in the province of Northland each year by police was up to NZ$700 million (£240 million/US$350 million) – one quarter of the region's gross domestic product. The report said: 'If you apply the rather optimistic assumption that the police manage to recover half of the annual crop, then clearly the industry is worth a great deal of money, probably more than the region's dairy industry.'

Several major cannabis growers learned their skills on horticultural courses sponsored by the government, the study said. One grower told a newspaper he had learned so much on the course he now grew, 'the best dope in Northland'.

NORWAY
Use is a criminal offence but authorities are often lenient and only impose a fine for small quantities. In extreme cases, offenders can be locked up for six months.

POLAND
In Poland it is legal to possess small amounts of cannabis for personal use.

PORTUGAL
Despite a reputation for being one of the most socially and religiously conservative countries in Europe, in July 2001 Portugal took everyone by surprise – not least its drug users – by decriminalizing the use of all narcotics, from cannabis to crack.

The reasoning behind the amazing move was summed up by Portugal's drugs tsar Vitalino Canas: 'Why not change the law to recognize that consuming drugs can be an illness or a route to illness? America has spent billions on enforcement but it has got nowhere. We view drug users as people who need help and care.'

Canas also pointed out that the police had already stopped arresting suspects and the courts were throwing out cases against users rather than sending them to jail for the maximum three year stint. Indeed, he claimed that prisons were merely a finishing school for drug addicts who wanted to become dealers. With Europe's worst drugs ghetto, the Casal Ventoso, slap bang in the middle of Lisbon, the evidence of Portugal's failure to stop the problem through traditional means is plain for all to see.

This has not stopped the country's ultra-conservative opposition party from wading in and issuing dire warnings about Europe's drug population arriving *en masse* in Portugal. 'We promise sun, beaches and any drug you like,' said Paulo Portas, leader of the Popular Party.

But the government insists that decriminalization is not the same as legalization. Drug use in Portugal is still punished under the new laws, but

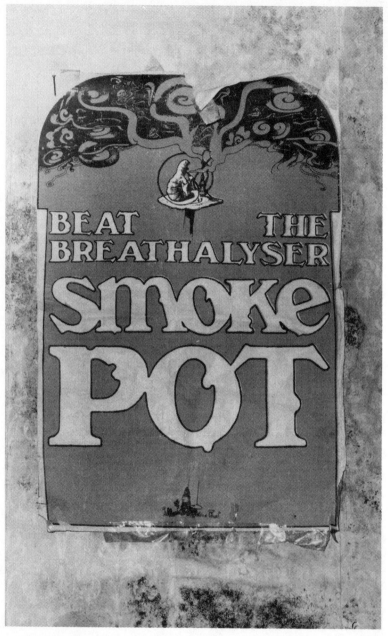

A 1969 poster offering alternatives to drink-driving.

"THE ACTUAL EXPERIENCE OF THE SMOKED HERB HAS BEEN CLOUDED BY A FOG OF UNRESPECTABILITY BY THE UNTHINKING, UNKNOLEGABLE FEW WHO HAVE NOT SMOKED THEM-SELVES AND YET INSIST UPON SETTING THEMSELVES UP AS CENTR-ES OF PROPAGANDA ABOUT THE SAID EXPERIENCE."

ALLEN GINSBERG.

Quote from the pro-marijuana American poet Allen Ginsberg, 1969.

once suspects have been arrested the responsibility is passed from the police to independent commissions who have the power to order fines, community service or detox programmes.

RUSSIA

Up until the 1970s, marijuana was only used in the remote Asian territories of the former Soviet Union. Most of the population preferred vodka. But the hippie revolution in the USA sent ripples as far as Moscow, and in certain bohemian circles it became *de rigueur* to smoke dope. Today, while alcohol is still the drug of choice among most Russians, almost all young people will admit to having smoked cannabis. They have also developed their own cannabis culture. For a start, instead of rolling the traditional spliff, they prefer to smoke 'papiroses' – short, stubby cigarettes without filters that are infiltrated with weed called 'kosyak'. In the southern regions there is even a popular drink consisting of marijuana boiled with milk fat and butter.

Conviction for buying or selling cannabis can result in imprisonment for between three and seven years. However, the low-paid Russian police are happy to accept bribes.

SINGAPORE

Adults caught trafficking more than 510g (8oz) of cannabis face the death penalty.

SPAIN

The Spanish authorities prohibit the personal use of cannabis but seldom prosecute for possession of small amounts – whether or not to arrest is left to the discretion of the police. Personal possession is now legally defined as up to 50g (1¾oz), but anything over that is considered to be a public health hazard.

SWEDEN

Of all of the European countries, Sweden has the harshest anti-cannabis legislation. Indeed, its attitude verges on the paranoid. In 1988 drug use was criminalized and in 1993 the penalty for drug consumption was increased to six months imprisonment. Police have the power to apprehend anyone they even think looks like they are under the influence of a drug and can take them to a police station and force them to undergo blood and urine tests.

SWITZERLAND

Concern is growing in Switzerland because a legal loophole allows cannabis to be cultivated openly on farms and sold over the counter or via the Internet as 'hemp'. Unlike most European countries, Switzerland allows cannabis to be grown legally while prohibiting its use as a drug. In the Alps, cannabis has enjoyed a revival among growers in recent years and is cultivated to produce textiles and cosmetics, to flavour food products and even to brew hemp beer. Dozens of hemp farms have sprung up in Switzerland in the past five years along with 150 hemp shops, where hemp products are sold together with marijuana. To cover themselves legally, the shops pack the dried weed in cellophane and then barcode, price and label it as 'hemp tea', 'dried flowers', 'organic buds' and 'scent sachets'. As a result, Switzerland has become Europe's biggest hemp producer, with 200 tons produced every year and a turnover of £200 million ($290 billion).

In 1999, one hemp trader was convicted by a Swiss court for selling drugs. But another court acquitted a fellow trader in a similar case while at the same time calling for clarity in the law. A recent report by the Federal Commission for Narcotics Issues, an independent panel that advises the government, found that half a million people out of Switzerland's population of seven million smoke cannabis at least once a month. The panel recommended legalizing possession, sale and consumption of small amounts within a strict legal framework. A decision is expected in 2003.

TURKEY

Punitive sentences are issued for anyone caught trafficking drugs.

'I won't go so far as saying cannabis actively damaged my health, but it decimated my record collection. I mean that literally. About six months after discovering the devil weed, I traded in my Beatles LPs for the soundtrack album of *The Harder They Come*.' - Toby Young, journalist

'The drug is really quite a remarkably safe one for humans, although it really is quite a dangerous one for mice and they should not use it.'
- JWD Henderson, director of the American Bureau of
Human Drugs, Health and Welfare

CANNABIS – THE NUTS AND BOLTS

Apart from its distinctive barbed leaves, the cannabis plant is strangely unremarkable and flimsy for one that has so successfully divided the world. In narcotic form, it assumes a totally different form. (This is made from the female plant as the male does not contain the necessary cannabinoids.) There are three distinct types:

- **Herbal** - The dried leaves and flowers of the plant. It is usually rolled in cigarette paper and smoked. Common street names: marijuana, grass, dope, draw, puff, blow, weed, gear, spliff, ganja, herb, wacky baccy, green, bud, skunk.
- **Resin** - Made by compressing the sap on the leaves and stems into blocks. Usually crumbled into tobacco, rolled and smoked. It can be eaten in cakes and biscuits. Common street names: hash, pot, dope, shit, black, gold, slate, squidgy.

- **Oil** – Formed when the resin is dissolved in a solvent and then allowed to evaporate. The oil can be then mixed with tobacco and smoked or it can be smeared on cigarette paper. Common street names: honey, oil, diesel.

THE DRUG AND HOW IT WORKS

The most active chemical in cannabis is delta9-tetrahydrocannabinol (THC). Cannabis creates a 'high' by affecting strategic locations in the brain, including:

- the hippocampus, where linear thinking takes place;
- the cerebellum, which co-ordinates movement and balance;
- the rostral ventromedial medulla, which modifies the intensity of pain sensations.

Recent research has identified natural brain chemicals similar to cannabinoids. Known as anandamides, these chemicals latch onto receptors in the brain to block pain and also help regular sleep patterns. THC latches onto the same receptors. Proponents of cannabis argue that THC is therefore utilizing existing pathways and does not contaminate the brain. Opponents claim that THC 'pirates' the brain's communication network, stealing receptors that should only be used by the brain's chemicals and therefore risking permanent changes to the brain's chemical make up. The fact that the cannabis debate cannot be resolved at its most basic level is also its most fundamental problem.

THE EFFECTS OF CANNABIS

When it comes to the effect of cannabis, whether psychological or physical, you can take your pick whose propaganda to believe. During the anti-marijuana purges of 1930s America, the official line was that cannabis was a menace that systematically turned the youth of the day into raving lunatics, mentally, physically and spiritually bankrupt and liable to commit heinous crimes at any time in order to feed their evil habit. Modern opponents are not quite so rabid, preferring instead to include cannabis within the general 'drugs menace' at large and, in particular, as a springboard to hard drugs such as heroin and cocaine.

'I once had what is known as "the horrors" when I had not been smoking long,' reported one case study in Berke and Hernton's *The Cannabis Experience*. 'The marijuana was a very strong variety, far stronger than anything I had ever smoked before, and I was in an extremely tense and unhappy personal situation. I lost all sense of time and place and had slight hallucinations – the walls came and went, objects and sounds were unreal and people looked like monsters. It was hard to breathe and I thought I was going to die and that no one would care. This feeling receded every now and then and I glimpsed reality. It lasted about half an hour and then I feel asleep.'

Equally, cannabis can appear to have absolutely no effect on some people. Tracey Bilton, 22, of London, said: 'I've tried it loads of times, but while all my mates were giggling away it just turned my eyeballs red. I think I'll stick to wine.'

Those in favour of cannabis, on the other hand, argue that not only is it a mellow, non-addictive high with no proven medical downside, but that 3,000 years' reliance upon its pharmaceutical properties are proof of its health benefits. 'At the end of a hard day, I like nothing better than coming home and lighting up a spliff,' says stockbroker Jared Hill, 28. 'It really relaxes me. I don't know what all the fuss about – you see these programmes like *The Good Life* where Jerry comes home and the first thing he does is pour himself a fucking enormous whisky. I mean, what's the difference?'

In the short term, the effect of cannabis depends largely upon the user's mental state before using, the environment and the user's expectations. Cannabis causes perceptual changes that make the user more aware of other peoples' feelings, enhance the enjoyment of music and give a general feeling of euphoria.

'I think the thing that pisses a lot of anti-cannabis people off is that they think people who smoke are just giggling idiots,' says barman Rudi Dale, 21. 'But they don't get it. I mean, what else can make you split your sides like that? I remember one time me and my buddy were stoned and we laughed for 20 minutes solid 'cos he'd dropped an egg on the floor. It's stupid I know, but I'd rather be laughing than be miserable. People need a laugh 'cos it's a tough life out there. I'm all for it.'

But cannabis can also make the user feel agitated and even paranoid if they are in a situation that is not pleasant – such as if they are with strangers or are trying to hide the fact that they are using it. In extreme moments, the user can feel that everything said around them is directed at them in a malicious and hurtful way.

'I just couldn't be doing with it,' says student Jane Peele. 'It made me on edge like you wouldn't believe. Everybody would be laughing and I'd be thinking they were laughing at me because I was stupid or because I was ugly or something like that. Even hours later the effects would still be there. I'd lie awake in a cold sweat, my heart racing, thinking that I was going to get into trouble because I'd smoked a joint. Now I just don't do it.'

Cannabis causes a number of physical changes including an increased pulse rate, a decrease in blood pressure, the alleviation of excess pressure in the eye, an opening of the airway leading to the lungs and suppression of the vomit reflex. But it can also produce bloodshot eyes, dry mouth, dizziness and an increased appetite – the dreaded 'munchies' in which a fridge full of food can be consumed in seconds. Sometimes short-term memory loss (ie the last couple of minutes) can also occur, although this passes as the effects of the drug wear off. However recent research by the McLean Hospital in Belmont, Massachusetts, found that mental function in heavy users was inhibited for 24 hours after the subjects had smoked pot – long after the high had gone.

Cannabis is also fat soluble, and so someone who regularly uses a large amount of the drug may store some of it in his or her body. It can take up to 30 days for this to be fully cleared by the body.

'IT'S NEVER KILLED NO ONE'

Cannabis aficionados boast that no one has ever been recorded as having died of an overdose. This may well be true: to fatally overdose on cannabis it is estimated that you would need to eat about 675g (24oz) of resin in one sitting – which is one big cake. To many experts, the problems with cannabis are less physical and more psychological and social. As Mark Kleiman, a drug policy expert from UCLA (University of California, Los Angeles) says: 'Smoking pot every third Saturday night isn't going to damage you in any measurable way, unless you do something stupid when you're stoned. The risk is that you won't be able to keep it to every third Saturday night.'

Since 1985, under the insistent leadership of the US, there has been a concerted campaign to control the international laundering of black-market money derived from drugs.

However, doctors point out that cannabis smoke contains many of the same toxic chemicals as tobacco smoke, including carcinogens such as tar, carbon monoxide and cyanide. Occasional users do not generally inhale enough smoke to affect the linings of the trachea and bronchial tubes. Heavy users, though, often experience the respiratory problems that 20-a-day cigarette smokers do, such as chronic bronchitis and the exacerbation of asthma. Small-scale studies of chronic cannabis-users' lungs have revealed abnormal changes in bronchial cells, indicating an increased risk of cancer, and many scientists believe that cannabis's lung-cancer risk could prove to be comparable to that of cigarettes.

Whether cannabis use leads to long-term health problems remains a bone of contention (see below). Suffice to say at this point, research for and against cannabis has proved frustratingly inconclusive, and the medical debate has become one of the most hotly contested in the weed's long history.

If a cannabis user does have an unpleasant experience when using the drug it is often the result of a high dose coupled with inexperience – perhaps after eating a large amount (ie more than 2g) and then panicking when the drug takes effect, or when cannabis is used with another drug such as alcohol.

THE HIGHS AND LOWS OF CANNABIS RESEARCH

In recent years, the call for the legalization of cannabis for medical use has gained substantial voice. In 2000, even British Prime Minister Tony Blair agreed that, in principle, there was a scientific case for decriminalization on medical grounds (see pp71–90 for a general look at the UK's recent cannabis history).

Popular opinion has also rapidly swung in the direction of legalization for medical purposes. In a British poll conducted in April 2000, 48 per cent of people supported the proposition that the Metropolitan Police should be persuaded to take no action against the medical use of cannabis. When the same poll was conducted in December of that same year, 71 per cent supported it.

By the time New Labour swept into its second term of office in May 2001, the perceived swing in political opinion, coupled with the unprecedented openness of public debate on the subject, made legalization of cannabis for medical use seem little more than a formality. All that was required was the rubber stamp of the government's trusted scientists to clear the way.

Unfortunately for the pro-legalizationists, science was providing anything but a united front in their favour. For every research project that concluded cannabis was a good thing, another claimed it was bad. Clinical trials at the James Paget Hospital in Norfolk, England, for instance, revealed that cannabis eased the suffering of 10 out of 13 multiple sclerosis victims.

'Cannabis is my Holy Grail,' says MS sufferer Claire Hodges. 'It's the only drug that works for me. I function properly when I have a smoke, I can see better, I have more energy, I can move more easily, I enjoy my food more and it even makes my bowels move better. It's as though MS sufferers are permanently below par and the high that you get from a little bit of cannabis brings you up to the point where you feel okay. Occasionally I get terrible attacks where I'm violently sick, shake and suffer vertigo. In those circumstances, my husband rolls me up a joint or I have it brewed as a cup of tea. The best medical advice comes from my dealer, who tells me to smoke little but often. It's as much a part of my life as eating three meals a day. With cannabis, I do my housework, talk to the kids and help them with their homework. Without a smoke, the quality of my life would deteriorate.'

At the same time, however, researchers at New Zealand's Asthma and Respiratory Foundation at Otago University, found that smoking cannabis five times a week does as much damage to the lungs as smoking 20 cigarettes a day. After examining the lungs of over 900 people aged 21, they concluded that smoking cannabis 'caused disease, phlegm and coughing fits'.

This problem seemed to be solved by scientists at Aberdeen University, Scotland, who revealed a new process whereby cannabis could be made soluble for the first time. This meant that instead of processing the drug along with other carcinogenic substances commonly found through smoking, cannabis could conceivably be delivered through sprays, injections or aerosols.

No sooner had this revelation raised the hopes of the pro-legalization lobby, then yet more research into the effects of the drug dealt them a double whammy. Scientists from Buffalo University in New York State claimed that cannabis included chemicals that, when smoked by either men or women, overloaded an important signalling system in the brain involved in fertility and reduced the chances of sperm breaking through the surface of an egg.

So not only did cannabis now make you infertile, it also made you a bad driver according to the UK's Transport Research Laboratory. While volunteers drove more slowly and cautiously when under the influence, their steering ability was badly affected – in particular, when trying to follow a figure-of-eight loop.

Meanwhile, researchers linked to the British-government-backed company GW Pharmaceuticals have been investigating 'soapbar', the most common grade of Moroccan hashish, so named because it is pressed into a shape like a bar of Imperial Leather soap (see pp115–16) for further details on GW). They have discovered that in many cases, 'soapbar' is impregnated with henna, coffee, diesel, boot polish, ghee and liquorice. In some extreme cases, traces of Largactil, a major tranquillizer, have been found.

The cause suffered an even more bizarre setback in September 2001, when British MP Angela Watkinson expressed concerns about the sheer mechanics of legalizing the drug after it was revealed certain members of the public were happily plundering fields of government-licensed cannabis being grown for research purposes near Upminster, Essex.

'When licences for the cultivation of this type of plant are granted then it should be on the condition that the premises being used are secure and that access by members of the public, and in particular to those wishing to sell this type of drug to others, is not possible,' said Mrs Watkinson. She then warned: 'One of the first areas that my committee will be considering is the likely effect of decriminalizing cannabis. This seems a classic example of what can happen.'

However there was some good news when, in January 2002, women in Britain's biggest trade union promoted cannabis as a calorie-free alternative to a glass of wine or a bar of chocolate. Calling for legalization of cannabis, a joint motion was debated at the Unison union's women's conference in Cardiff, Wales, when delegates representing 900,000 women claimed it was crucial that women should be able to escape the growing tensions of working life. 'Cannabis can be used for women to relax without calories, in contrast to alcohol or chocolate,' said the motion. There was even a solution for those who do not smoke. Non-smokers can use cannabis by incorporating it into recipes and cooking with it, added the motion, in possible contradiction of the calorie-free argument.

> Like alcohol, even moderate use of cannabis impedes a person's ability to learn, operate machinery, or drive a vehicle.

Despite this, with New Labour firmly ensconced in their second term, the road to the medical legalization of cannabis seems as tortuous as a figure-of-eight loop, and just as difficult to steer, as far as frustrated campaigners are concerned.

CANNABIS – GATEWAY DRUG TO THE HARD STUFF?

In 1939, Dr James C Munch, the US Official Expert on marihuana from 1938–62, testified in court, under oath, that marijuana had turned him into a bat. Dr Munch also supported the testimony of one murder defendant who claimed insanity because he had been in the same room with a bag of marijuana. The defendant was later acquitted by reason of marijuana-induced insanity.

Such was the level of the attacks against cannabis during the Anslinger-led persecution of the 1930s. But one area of propaganda that remains an important tenet of the anti-cannabis lobby to this day is the suggestion that cannabis is but the first step on the ladder to addiction to hard drugs like heroin.

Initially, not even Anslinger believed there was a link. Indeed in the 1920s, some US states outlawed marijuana because of the belief that heroin addiction would lead to the use of marijuana. In 1937, Anslinger testified before Congress that there was no connection at all between marijuana and heroin. The reason marijuana had to be outlawed, he said, was because it caused insanity, criminality and death. One example he gave was of two young lovers who became so crazed after smoking a joint that they eloped and got married. The hemp industry representatives who also testified were uniformly surprised and mystified to hear that a dangerous drug could be made from this widespread and common crop. And, in 1944, the La Guardia Committee Report on Marijuana agreed there was no connection at all between cannabis and heroin.

In 1951, however, Anslinger suddenly, and apparently on the spot, changed his mind when, testifying once again for a stepping up of the anti-cannabis laws, he asserted that marijuana was the certain stepping stone to heroin addiction. It has been the basis of US marijuana policy ever since, despite statistical evidence to the contrary.

In 1970, the Canadian government did their largest study ever of the subject and found no connection between marijuana and heroin. In 1972, the US government did their own study and again found no connection between marijuana and heroin. This was also the conclusion of the largest study ever carried out by the American Consumers Union, published in the same year.

Subsequent studies in both America and the UK have failed to find any solid evidence of a link, although in the last few years, as the laws on the use of cannabis have been loosened in the UK, fears have inevitably been articulated that it will result in more young people moving onto heroin. Former drugs tsar Keith Hellawell was one of those who warned of the dangers, claiming that research from New Zealand proved that youngsters who smoked cannabis were 60 times more likely to move onto the hard stuff.

By far the most interesting comment, however, has come from literary drugs guru Irvine Welsh, author of *Trainspotting*. 'I'd always done a lot of sniffing glue as a kid,' he said. 'And then I went onto lager and speed. I drifted into heroin because as a kid growing up everybody told me, "don't smoke marijuana, it will kill you". '

RECENT UK HASH HISTORY

As we have seen, although it had been available for over a century, and its therapeutic use promoted by luminaries such as Queen Victoria's private physician, prescription cannabis was withdrawn as part of the 1971 Misuse of Drugs Act. But in the late 1990s, medical research and increased lobbying by Multiple Sclerosis suffers in particular, led to a reappraisal of the official line.

In 1997, the British Medical Association (BMA) acknowledged the therapeutic benefits of cannabis, but expressed concern that joints containing tobacco cause more lung damage than cigarettes. In the same year Home Secretary Jack Straw gave GW Pharmaceuticals a licence to grow cannabis, acknowledging that an extract could become available on prescription. And in 1998 the House of Lords called for the government to allow doctors to prescribe cannabis for medical use.

In 1999, after testing different strains of hash, GW Pharmaceuticals claimed *cannabis sativa*, normally grown for its flowers rather than its resin, was the most effective pain-relieving strain.

By 2000, the first study proving that cannabis eases the symptoms of MS had been published in the science journal *Nature*. Scientists in London, Aberdeen and South Carolina reported that they had direct proof that a cannabinoid compound used on mice with an MS-like condition helped ameliorate symptoms within minutes.

When newly appointed Home Secretary David Blunkett reclassified cannabis to a Class C drug in 2001, he refused to legalize it for medical use until tests were complete. Meanwhile, the first clinical trials pronounced cannabis to be a 'wonder drug' capable of radically transforming the lives of very sick people. Preliminary results of the UK government trial suggested that 80 per cent of those taking part derived more benefit from cannabis than from any other drug, with many describing it as 'miraculous'.

In 2002, scientists discovered a natural brain molecule that mimics the effects of cannabis. The find should help researchers to develop pharmaceuticals with the therapeutic effects of the drug but without the 'high' and unwanted side effects.

THE US MEDICAL DEBATE

In the United States, the movement to legalize cannabis for medicinal purposes has been gradually cranked up from state to state. According to a poll taken in 1999, 73 per cent of Americans support the use of marijuana as a physician-prescribed pain reliever. In 1990, a survey revealed that 44 per cent of American oncologists had suggested that a patient smoke marijuana for relief of the nausea caused by chemotherapy. In 1997, the American Medical Association recommended controlled clinical trials on the medical uses of smoked marijuana. Meanwhile products using synthetic cannabinoids are selling well in the United States. The annual sales of dronabil – a synthetic cannabinoid sold under the trade name of Marinol – are estimated to be worth $20 million (£13.8 million) in the US. Around 80 per cent of the prescriptions are as appetite stimulants for people with AIDS or HIV, 10 per cent to counteract the nausea associated with chemotherapy and 10 per cent for other purposes. Meanwhile, the Eli Lilly Company has developed nabilone. Under the trade name Cesamet, it too is used to counter nausea brought on by chemotherapy as well as treating patients with anxiety problems.

But, as in the UK, American campaigners have found the authorities – both at state and federal level – unwilling to commit themselves to a relaxation of the current laws. In many cases, the laws of the individual states differ to a confusing degree, and there is always the spectre of the ultra-conservative Drugs Enforcement Administration on hand to clamp down on anything it perceives as illegal.

This, however, has not stopped dozens of so-called 'cannabis clubs' from springing up. These are places where sufferers of everything from multiple sclerosis to AIDS regularly turn up to smoke cannabis. A typical example is the Los Angeles Cannabis Resource Center. The centre boasts its own indoor plantation where over 400 plants are grown under lights. Upstairs is a comfortable lounge where 833 patients with a range of illnesses are invited to smoke the drug to alleviate the nausea and pain associated with their treatment. A patient needs a recommendation from a physician to become a member of the centre, and before the centre gives the patient marijuana it requires the doctor's certification that there is a legitimate need and also checks that the physician is licensed by the state.

The centre was set up in 1996, following a ruling by nine US states – Alaska, Arizona, California, Colorado, Hawaii, Maine, Nevada, Oregon and Washington – that allows patient use of marijuana. But, such is the capricious nature of state versus federal law, it and other cannabis clubs could soon be shut down. In May 2001, the US Supreme Court ordered that a club in nearby Oakland must stop dispensing cannabis. This followed a ruling by Justice Clarence Thomas that federal laws prohibiting the manufacture and distribution of marijuana had to take precedence over a patient's medical need for the drug.

While that decision did not overturn California's own decision to allow the seriously ill to possess and use marijuana with a physician's approval, and while federal agencies have yet to act against them, the court has provided federal prosecutors with hefty ammunition against the cannabis clubs. It has also given anti-drugs organizations something to get their teeth into. 'If you make drugs more socially acceptable, use starts to rise,' said Howard Simon, a spokesman for Partnership for a Drug-Free America. 'Kids may be able to make a distinction, but they may not.' They point out that under the Controlled Substances Act of 1970, cannabis is a potentially addictive drug with no medical value.

Members of the cannabis clubs have been predictably bullish about the threat, pointing out that only two months after the Supreme Court decision, the Canadians began allowing seriously ill people to buy, cultivate and use marijuana to alleviate their symptoms. And like their counterparts in the UK, American campaigners have found support from government.

Democrat Congressman Barney Frank has called on Congress to reclassify cannabis so that it can be distributed on prescription. 'Marijuana and the people who use it are treated far more harshly than the actual substance justifies,' he said. 'We allow doctors to prescribe substances that are far more damaging.' But even Frank is pessimistic after the Supreme Court's ruling. 'With that ruling in their pocket, they could bring injunctive actions against every club they could find.'

Not only that, but the DEA are taking a typically hard line on the issue. 'Marijuana is illegal, and any place that distributes marijuana, that grows marijuana, is illegal under federal law,' said a spokesman.

When police raided an apartment in Capitol Hill, Washington in 1975, it was what they discovered growing in pots on the next-door neighbour's porch that interested them more. Investigations proved conclusive and, sure enough, when the owner of the flat, 27-year-old teacher Robert Randall, returned from a vacation with his girlfriend, he found himself under arrest for cultivating marijuana.

Thus began one of the most controversial and significant episodes in US cannabis history. For instead of admitting the charge, Randall told the court that he smoked marijuana to alleviate the symptoms of glaucoma from which he had suffered for years. He had first discovered the curative powers of the drug in 1973 and now, he claimed, it was the only thing that stopped him from going blind.

At first, even Randall's lawyer laughed at the audacity of the claim. But Randall was deadly serious, and subjected himself to a battery of tests conducted by a researcher from UCLA to support his claims. In November 1976, a Superior Court Judge ruled that Randall had 'established a defence of necessity... The evil he sought to avert, blindness, is greater than that he performed.' The charges were dismissed, and at that moment Randall became forever known as the man who began the movement to legalize marijuana for medical purposes.

Randall took his new role seriously. After successfully petitioning the Food and Drug Administration, he was included in a research program that allotted him ten marijuana joints a day. The marijuana was grown at a University of Mississippi farm, rolled into cigarettes at a facility in North Carolina and shipped in a tin to pharmacies near Randall's home. He said that he never got high from the marijuana, since he smoked so much of it. He also was critical of the government drug's characteristics, saying it was 'consistently bad... very metallic. It lacks the fine, almost perfumed taste of street marijuana.'

From then until his death from AIDS in 2001, Randall was a familiar figure in courtrooms across the USA, mainly as a representative of the group he founded, the Alliance for Cannabis Therapeutics. He featured predominantly in a number of landmark cases. In 1987 he was a key witness in a two-year public hearing into the question of whether the DEA should reclassify marijuana as a Schedule II drug that could be prescribed by physicians. The DEA denied the petition.

In the early 1990s, Randall established the Marijuana AIDS Research Service, which helped AIDS patients apply for the medicinal cannabis programme. Closure of this programme led activists to turn to the polls and sponsor various state ballot initiatives, including California's Proposition 215, which allowed for medical use of marijuana.

Moreover, Randall was determined that medical use of marijuana should not be confused with those who wanted it legalized for recreational purposes. 'Seriously ill Americans are caught in the crossfire as drug warriors on both sides of the cultural divide try to turn the sick into cannon fodder,' he said.

THE CANADIAN ENLIGHTENMENT

As campaigners around the world fight what they see as intransigent governments to get marijuana legalized for medical use, many cast an envious glance at unfashionable Canada. For, in July 2001, Canada became the first country in the world to do just that.

Indeed, the sweeping nature of their legislation means that use of the drug is not solely restricted to sprays or pills containing cannabinoids extracts. In Canada – as long as you've got a doctor's certificate and testaments from two legal witnesses that you have either a terminal illness,

AIDS, arthritis, cancer, multiple sclerosis, epilepsy or degenerative muscle and bone disease – you can grow it, smoke it, eat it or put it in pies. It's entirely up to you. You can even get someone to grow your hash for you.

Such is the progressive nature of Canada's cannabis legislation, the country's Supreme Court has agreed to hear arguments that criminalization of the weed is unconstitutional on the grounds that it poses no significant health risk. Meanwhile, in the depths of a disused mineshaft in Manitoba, the government have funded an enormous cannabis plantation designed to produce 185kg (400lb) a week for use in medical experiments.

THE MYSTERIOUS WORLD OF GW PHARMACEUTICALS

They are described as a 'cross between a spaceship and an operating theatre' and, unless you have the required strict clearance, that description is the nearest you will ever get to the greenhouses of GW Pharmaceuticals. For it is in these hi-tech greenhouses, situated in a heavily guarded, secret location in the south of England, that more than 40,000 man-sized cannabis plants are being grown under computer-controlled conditions. And despite the cloak-and-dagger approach, the cannabis here is being grown with the blessing of the British government.

GW Pharmaceuticals is the country's largest licensed grower of cannabis, and its on-going mission is to develop prescription drugs using the medical properties of cannabinoids, the molecules unique to the cannabis plant that have been shown to have analgesic, anti-convulsant, anti-tremor, anti-psychotic, anti-inflammatory, anti-emetic and appetite-stimulant properties.

For the last five years, GW's scientists have been working at developing a range of products targeted at multiple sclerosis, spinal cord injury, neurogenic pain, spasticity and other neurological dysfunction, arthritis, migraine, head injury, schizophrenia, weight loss associated with cancer and AIDS and chemotherapy-induced nausea and vomiting. The company's founder, former hospital doctor Geoffrey Guy, has lobbied the government to permit prescriptions of cannabis-based drugs, and claims that the Home Office has pledged that if GW's clinical trials are successful, it will reschedule cannabis to permit its use in pharmaceuticals.

Commander Brian Paddick of the Metropolitan Police, the UK's highest-ranking openly gay policeman, was removed from his job after being accused of smoking cannabis. Paddick first came to public notice when he liberalized the policing of cannabis laws in Brixton to allow officers to concentrate on the trade in crack cocaine and heroin.

Anita Roddick, founder of green cosmetics chain the Body Shop, defended her chain's launch of a range of products based on the cannabis plant, saying it is a versatile plant which has little or nothing to do with drug abuse: 'Vilifying hemp because of marijuana is like vilifying potatoes because of vodka.'

Howard Marks, widely regarded as the number one cannabis trafficker of the 1970s and 1980s. Oxford educated, Marks built up a worldwide smuggling network, supplying the majority of marijuana smoked in the western world. By the mid-1980s, he owned 25 companies, possessed 43 aliases, and is estimated to have made more than £48 million ($70 million) from his trafficking activities.

Cheech Marin and Tommy Chong, who in the 1970s took marijuana's laid back, spaced-out culture and milked it for laughs on record and in the movies. Their 1972 debut album, *Cheech And Chong*, was a hit and was followed by several others, including *Big Bambu* and *Los Cochinos*, while in 1978 the duo made their movie breakthrough in *Up In Smoke*, which proved to be a box-office smash.

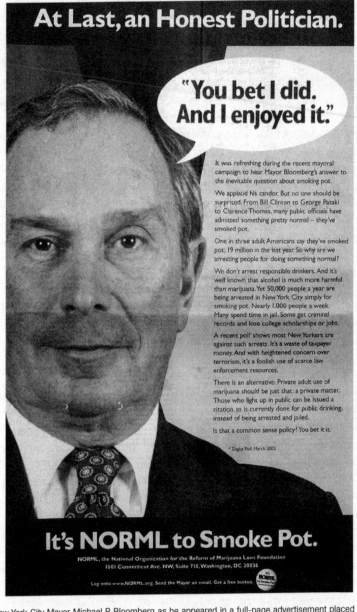

New York City Mayor Michael R Bloomberg as he appeared in a full-page advertisement placed in *The New York Times* on 9 April 2002 by the National Organization for the Reform of Marijuana Laws Foundation (NORML). The Washington-based group sought to dissuade the New York City government from arresting people for smoking marijuana. The quote by Bloomberg is from a remark made to a reporter in 2001, before he announced that he was running for Mayor.

Patients in the trials programme take different formulations of cannabis-based medicines by means of a sub-lingual spray device - it is sprayed under the tongue and absorbed, rather than swallowed. The patients also take an inactive 'placebo'. Neither the researchers nor the patients know whether they are using the active substance or the placebo at any given time. According to Dr Guy, results from his clinical trials to date have been encouraging, with patients showing 'significant reduction in pain, muscle spasm and bladder dysfunction as well as improved neurological function'.

'Data from our studies in approximately 70 subjects is positive and encouraging,' he said. 'Patients are clearly gaining benefit. These results provide enough confidence for us to increase the number of trial centres and the number of patients taking part. We are seeing a significant improvement in quality of life for sufferers of a range of medical conditions and look forward to extending the trials programme.'

In 2001, GW began clinical trials at Ottawa Hospital in Canada. This is because the change in legislation now means that Canada allows sufferers from chronic conditions such as multiple sclerosis and arthritis to apply, to possess and to cultivate cannabis for medical purposes legally.

CANNABIS – WORSE FOR YOU THAN YOU EVER IMAGINED!

There are lies and statistics... And when it comes to an issue as controversial as cannabis, statistics can be found to bolster either side's argument. Even as the pro-cannabis lobby were beginning to get their message across about the medicinal advantages of the drug, the anti-lobby were dredging up alternative research that proved their point. For example, researchers in Boston announced in 2001 that the risk of a heart attack goes up nearly five times in the first hour after smoking a joint. For someone in their 20s, the risk is so low to begin with that it remains insignificant. But for older people, a factor of five could mean trouble. 'People's risk for coronary artery disease increases as they enter their 40s and 50s, so the risks associated with smoking marijuana, which might have been a trivial issue when people were younger, may now pose a significant health concern,' said the lead researcher Murray Mittleman, director of cardiovascular epidemiology at Boston's Beth Israel Deaconess medical centre.

The report made good headline propaganda – but between the lines the argument was less than watertight. The researchers admitted that smoking a joint puts no more extra strain on the heart than strenuous physical exercise, which is universally recommended as being good for you. Another catch in the research was that it was based on interviews with people who had just survived heart attacks, and did not look at the relative cardiac health of cannabis smokers versus non-users in the population as a whole. Of the 3,882 interviewees, only 3 per cent admitted to having used cannabis in the year before their heart attack, and only 0.2 per cent – nine people – smoked it in the hour before.

But even as this was being dismissed as hysterical overreaction, another grim warning was issued. A team from Buffalo University declared that attacks of 'the munchies' – the phenomenon associated with smoking cannabis that results in late-night trips to the corner shop to stock up on crisps, peanuts, cakes, chocolate and fizzy drinks – may have serious long-term health consequences for frequent users. More than 11,000 users and non-users between the ages of 20 and 59 were interviewed, given physical examinations and asked to fill in questionnaires on foods eaten recently and regularly. Blood chemistry tests were also done. The study found that users ate fewer fruits and vegetables and therefore had lower levels of essential antioxidants in their blood. Marijuana is also thought to have a detrimental effect on levels of vitamins and minerals. Users also drank more beer, spirits and high-calorie drinks. 'These lifestyle habits could increase the risk for chronic diseases such as heart disease and cancer in the long term,' said Dr Ellen Smit, the study's lead author.

THE 'BENEFICIAL HERB' – THE SO-CALLED ETHICAL DRUGS TRADE

In 1999, as part of a BBC television documentary series called *Living With The Enemy*, a Conservative student politician went to Brixton, South London, to live with a group of ganja-smoking Rastas during the annual Legalize Cannabis Rally. He was supposed to stay there for a week but, after only one night, he packed his bags and legged it to the nearest police station in order to register a complaint.

In line with the local police chief's policy in the Brixton area, no action was taken – much to the young Conservative's spluttering outrage. The sudden relaxation in cannabis policing in certain districts such as Brixton and nearby Lambeth is symptomatic of the widespread unclenching of establishment buttocks when it comes to perceptions of the drug itself, and in particular its health benefits. While the government 'ums and aahs' about whether to legalize cannabis for medical usage, others have already made their minds up. In one of a series of landmark court cases that same year, multiple sclerosis sufferer Lezley Gibson, from Cumbria, was cheered to the rafters at Carlisle Crown Court when, after admitting smoking up to five joints a day to ease her symptoms, she was acquitted of criminal possession of drugs by a jury. Afterwards, 36-year-old Mrs Gibson said she would continue smoking cannabis and called for a change in the law: 'There are hundreds of people like me out there,' she said. ' No one in my position should have to be dragged through the courts like this, but I am glad it is all over. I feel brilliant.'

She told the court she began smoking at the age of 24, three years after being diagnosed with MS. She had tried other medications and treatments, but nothing made her feel as well as cannabis. She smoked up to five joints a day bought from dealers, because it enabled her to have a more normal life. 'I would use paint stripper if I thought it would make me well,' she said.

In the 2001 General Election Lezley's husband Mark was one of dozens of candidates who stood for the Legalize Cannabis Alliance. Although he was never in danger of winning, he received 870 votes – a result mirrored in constituencies across the country.

But it is no longer simply multiple sclerosis sufferers and their supporters who are advocating cannabis use. Prince Charles even laid his cards on the table when he told one MS sufferer that he'd 'heard it was the best thing' to relieve the symptoms.

The message about medicinal marijuana, particularly for the relief of MS symptoms, is one that is being promoted across the world. In Japan, where the drug is outlawed, businessman Kendo Ogasawara is campaigning to allow patients in need of relief legal access to the medicine that has helped him. He is one of the founders of the Japanese Association for Medical Marijuana, JAMM, a non-profit group formed for just that purpose. Ogasawara, a 34-year-old Tokyo businessman, was diagnosed with multiple sclerosis five years ago. 'If cannabis helps relieve these terrible symptoms, then why shouldn't we be allowed to use it?' he said.

'We are not dealers or traffickers, we are just ordinary people who want to ease our suffering.'

The official report from the Advisory Council on the Misuse of Drugs (ACMD), commissioned by Home Secretary David Blunkett in October 2001, comes out firmly in favour of downgrading cannabis from Class B to Class C legal status but warns that it is not a harmless drug.

Meanwhile Harvard University medical professor Dr Lester Grinspoon, author of two well known books about marijuana, is leading the charge in the United States and claims to have strong evidence for a variety of medical applications of marijuana: it reduces nausea and vomiting associated with cancer chemotherapy and treatment of AIDS symptoms, it reverses weight loss experienced by many AIDS patients, it helps to control epileptic seizures, it relieves severe symptoms of glaucoma and it alleviates the muscle spasms associated with multiple sclerosis and paraplegia and quadriplegia.

By the turn of the century, a void had been created by the general public's growing confidence in cannabis as a beneficial herb and the increasingly *laissez-faire* attitude of the authorities towards prosecution. It was not long before entrepreneurial spirit filled the gap in the market, in the shape of 'ethical' drugs traders.

A typical example is Tony Taylor, a health food shop owner based in King's Cross, London. Taylor openly imports cannabis from farmers in Switzerland – both buds and hashish – and sells it to more than 200 medical patients at cost price in the form of hemp cream, a tincture that can be dropped into water for MS patients and even a preparation made during a full moon for women with PMT.

'We have a protocol,' he says. 'We fill in a form, you get interviewed by me. I don't charge anything for consultation.' Under the 1971 Misuse of Drugs Act, Taylor could be imprisoned for up to 14 years. Yet the local police turn a blind eye. Taylor believes the reason for this is because of his 'ethical' stance towards the sale of the drug.

'I can see it from both points of view,' he says. 'I see it from the establishment point of view: if you have totally free everything, it seems people will want to abuse it totally. I don't advocate smoking ganja at work, and a lot of people become, on cannabis, like they are with alcohol. I've been there myself. But fortunately it isn't addictive, so it's a bit easier to get off it. From a stress point of view, it's very good – but it's about dosage, like any medicine.'

The reason Taylor makes regular trips to Switzerland for his supplies is that Alpine cannabis farmers can grow it in their fields with impunity. Although it is currently sold in Swiss hemp shops, a government advisory committee there has recommended that it should be sold in pharmacies on a non-profit basis – a situation that Tony Taylor and others would like to see in the UK.

Unfortunately, while the police in King's Cross are prepared to allow Taylor to sell his illegal wares without interference, other forces have proved somewhat more intransigent. In April 2000, Lancashire Police were criticized for their treatment of great-grandmother Jean Jackson. In the six months since she had been smoking cannabis to ease her arthritis, Miss Jackson's antiques shop in Lancaster had been raided six times. On the last occasion, she gave officers a key to let themselves in after ten detectives proceeded to take apart the sewage pipes in her home.

'A number of officers go to carry out searches of this kind and when searching for drugs it is common practice to make a rapid entry,' explained Chief Superintendent John Thompson. 'Possession of cannabis is an offence and if people are in possession they can expect to be prosecuted.'

Colin Davies, who set up the Medical Marijuana Co-operative, slammed police tactics. 'The police have been a bit heavy-handed by turning up in this jack-booted fashion to tread on ill people,' he said. 'It is bizarre the way they pick out people who are ill, who are like sitting ducks, and they do not actually check whether these people have reasons in the first place.'

During a visit to a day care centre in Cheltenham, Gloucestershire, in December 1998, the Prince met MS sufferer Karen Drake. Asking about her health, he inquired whether she had experimented with alternative remedies to deal with her crippling pain.

Ms Drake, 36, said: 'He asked me if I had tried taking cannabis, saying he understood that, under strict medical supervision, it was one of the best things for it. I was surprised that he asked me, but it was nice of him to be so considerate. It showed that he had thought about the condition and knew what was helpful.'

Charles' comments were gleefully seized upon by campaigners for legalization like Labour MP Paul Flynn, who said: 'It is splendid advice from a most unexpected source. I am encouraged to learn that the high level of popular support for the use of cannabis for medicinal purposes has reached Buckingham Palace.'

A Royal spokesman was more circumspect when asked about the Prince's comments. 'Prince Charles is aware of the issue of the use of cannabis for MS sufferers. Health is one of his major portfolios, and I think people would be surprised if he wasn't aware of the debate on the treatment of MS sufferers.'

MONEY

'If there is one entrepreneur in the cannabis market who has always kept his head on his shoulders it is Ben Dronkers. This small and calm 48-year-old man is the owner of a true cannabis growing and trading empire with a turnover of 4 to 6 million Dutch florins per year and more than an additional million for paraphernalia, but these numbers are judged as an underestimation by many officials. But Dronkers hastens to add: "I'm just a hippie trying to appear serious in a conventional Dutch way. In fact, there is a much stronger and more fundamental inner link that binds me to cannabis."' - Report in *Le Monde*, 1998

For such a little plant, cannabis is truly big business. But then, for all the talk of the history and culture of the drug, it remains just that: a drug. A soft one in some eyes perhaps, but a drug nonetheless and as lucrative to manufacturers and dealers as any other. Before it reaches the rolling papers of millions of smokers, cannabis is still subjected to a complex and secretive smuggling process that takes it from the growing fields of the Middle East and South America across the borders of dozens of countries in which the penalties for trafficking are severe. It might not have the kudos of cocaine and heroin in the eyes of the drugs authorities, but every year they still crack down with all their resources on those responsible for its production and distribution. And as long as cannabusiness remains highly profitable to the criminal underworld, the battle will continue.

In March 2000 detectives arrested four people following a raid on one of Britain's best-organized cannabis production factories. Several hundred high-strength skunk cannabis plants - with a crop worth £500,000

($725,000) – were found growing in the old aircraft hangar at an industrial estate at Breighton, near York. The plants were almost ready for harvest but some had already been picked and were being dried.

Meanwhile in June 2000, police in Rotterdam arrested 16 people after a crop worth almost £1 million ($1.5 million) was discovered in a series of plastic greenhouses on the outskirts of the city.

Cigarette firms anticipating legalisation have already registered brand names with links to marijuana. In 1993, Philip Morris filed a trade-mark application in France for 'Marley'. The firm later denied this link. Other drug-related names registered by companies include Acapulco Gold and Red Leb.

'It's a pain when they catch you, because it takes a lot of time and effort to set up a weed production site,' said Mick, a convicted supplier from East Anglia. 'But if you're bright, you'll have more than one site on the go at any one time. I know guys who have tipped off the police about one of their own sites, just to keep them from getting near the bigger ones. It's a business, and a good one at that. You're not going to let it go just like that, are you? Anyway, I don't see why some multinational should get millions of pounds from the government for growing cannabis and we get locked away. If it's illegal, it should be illegal for everyone.'

But Mick and his cannabis-growing compatriots are merely small fry compared to the global trafficking trade.

ALL ROADS LEAD TO AMSTERDAM

The Dutch authorities turn a deliberately blind eye to cannabis. But while this largely unique attitude of tolerance makes the cannabis cafés of Amsterdam a magnet for pot-heads from all over the world, it leaves Europe's drug squads with an enduring headache. Amsterdam and Dutch ports like Rotterdam and Europort have become a gateway for the drugs trade, and Holland is the major distribution centre for the international trafficking of narcotics including cannabis throughout western Europe and, in particular, Britain.

In 1998, the UK accounted for more than a fifth of cannabis seizures within the 15 member states of the European Union. It's a short hop across the North Sea for British dealers to meet up with like-minded gangs of smugglers from all of the major European capitals, and there is no way the thin blue line of customs officials and drug squad officers can keep tabs on the thousands of consignments of cannabis, ranging from a few grams to several hundred kilos, that arrive in Britain every week.

'It's like trying to keep back the tide,' said one British customs official. 'You think you've done well stopping one consignment coming in from the continent, then it quickly dawns on you that while you've been patting yourself on the back another six have come in under your nose.'

Cannabis resin, the form most widely used in the UK, traditionally comes from the so-called Golden Crescent of countries, which includes Morocco, Afghanistan and Pakistan. It is also highly prevalent in Asia, especially in Cambodia where the Khmer Rouge sanctioned huge production sites for drug cartels from Sweden, China and Thailand. Consignments from South American countries such as Venezuela and Colombia are regularly shipped into the European ports.

According to the International Narcotics Control Strategy Report of 2000: 'While Cambodia is not a major producer of opiates or coca-based drugs, marijuana is cultivated in significant quantities for export, mainly to Europe... Poorly paid and ill-trained police and judicial officials frequently look the other way in narcotics and other criminal cases.'

Commercial cannabis is grown and processed on an industrial scale. In Afghanistan, the narcotics industry was the primary source of income for the ruling Taliban government and, intelligence sources believe, the al-Qua'eda terrorist organization of Osama Bin Laden that was based there. Following the destruction of the World Trade Centre on 11 September 2001, many of the subsequent US and British attacks on Afghanistan were aimed at disrupting and destroying this link.

Cannabis shipments follow a route up through Turkey and eastern Europe to the main trafficking centres of Germany and Holland. Generally the crops are cultivated and processed by peasants who, depending on the demand, either turn the cannabis into resin or grass. Of the billions of pounds their labours will eventually realize, most will get peanuts. It is, however, their living – and while hard-hitting government clampdowns on cannabis production in some countries have disrupted the trafficker, the real effect has been felt by the farmers who are left penniless.

When Lebanon wiped out the Bekaa valley's $500 million (£345 million)-a-year cannabis industry in the 1990s, it was a catastrophe for the impoverished area. But farmers in this remote area have decided that there is nothing for it but to crank up production of the drug once again, believing that risking the wrath of the authorities is better than starving to death. In 2001, according to reliable estimates, 6,000ha (15,000 acres) of cannabis were planted – by far the largest amount since the Lebanese government began its eradication programme ten years ago at the end of the civil war. The rewards are great: a single hectare can reap £14,000 ($20,000) for the farmer – which is why Dr Mohammed Ferjani, the Tunisian head of the Bekaa's UN-sponsored integrated rural development programme, predicts a full-scale rebellion if the illicit crops are destroyed. 'The people are obliged to search for a cash crop to ensure a respectable income,' he says. 'This year, I'm sure they will fight.'

BLACK IN THE USSR – THE DRUGS EXPLOSION IN THE FORMER COMMUNIST STATES

The fall of the Soviet Union and the disintegration of its empire into separate states known as the Central Independent States (CIS) was greeted with unbridled joy in the west. But less than ten years after the death of communism, western governments are discovering that its legacy has a bitter taste. For no one celebrated the new freedoms in the eastern bloc more than the drugs cartels, who gleefully turned parts of the former USSR into a drugs production and trafficking centre that has now superseded the traditional heartlands of Asia and the Middle East.

In 1999, police in Primoriye discovered more than 120 cannabis fields covering close to 100ha (250 acres). This followed hot on the heels of the discovery of 200ha (500 acres) of cannabis in the Khabarovsk region. Although arrests were made, drug enforcement agencies acknowledge that this is merely the tip of the iceberg.

Communist leaders in the Soviet Union and eastern Europe formerly believed that illegal drugs trafficking was a problem that belonged to the decadent western capitalists. As a result, when the Soviet Bloc collapsed, the authorities in former communist states found themselves woefully lacking in the training and expertise to deal both with drug users and traffickers.

Drug use is not a crime in the Czech Republic, Kazakhstan, Poland, the Russian Federation, Slovakia or Turkmenistan. In Poland, existing penalties for trafficking are rarely imposed, while in the Czech Republic and Slovakia it is completely legal to cultivate cannabis, and seeds are sold openly in local shops.

The sheer scale of cannabis availability in the east compounds the problem. It is estimated that more than 1 million ha (2½ million acres) of mostly wild cannabis grows throughout the CIS. A report by a visiting UN team in 1992 revealed that in Kazakhstan and Krygyzstan alone there were more than 200,000ha (500,000 acres) of cannabis plantations – more than five times the recorded marijuana cultivation in the rest of the world.

Drug syndicates have been quick to exploit both the natural abundance of cannabis and the incompetence of the local authorities. They are able to set up harvesting and processing plants largely with impunity. And, once the cannabis has been processed, the absence of any centralized or cohesive drug enforcement in eastern and central Europe makes it easy to traffick the finished product to the greedy markets of the west. Where once the primary conduit for cannabis trafficking used to be Turkey, the authorities are beginning to realise that the drug is now flooding into France, Holland and Germany from Poland. With largely non-existent trafficking laws, Polish gangs have flourished. It is thought that much of the drugs currently reaching western markets come through the so-called Polish Pipeline – a broad network of Polish gangsters who serve as links in the wholesale trade of Central Asian hashish, Afghan heroin or even Colombian cocaine, receiving the drugs from Poland and selling them to local dealers.

The fact that drug smuggling from east to west is hardly sophisticated indicates the derision with which the major drugs gangs regard the authorities. Recent busts by Polish and Czechoslovakian police found cannabis hidden in a shipment of beans, and another load disguised as a pineapple shipment. Neither haul was more than a few hundred kilos – peanuts compared to the vast amounts of the drug that pass unmolested every day.

While busts are an inconvenience, traffickers are more than happy to endure the occasional set back as long as the trade remains so lucrative. It has been estimated that for every £10 ($14.50) of hash bought on the street, around £6 ($8.70) of that goes to the trafficker, compared to £1 ($1.45) to the grower, £1 ($1.45) to the dealer and £2 ($2.90) in 'administration' incurred by the various stages of its transport.

And it is not only crime syndicates who recognize the money-spinning opportunities of the drugs trade. Almost all the major terrorist groups in the world rely on trafficking in some form as a means of fund raising. While initially it was South American insurgents such as the Revolutionary Armed Forces of Colombia who exploited drug money, their lead has been followed by other groups across the world such as Peru's Shining Path, the IRA and the Kurdish Workers Party in Turkey. Even religious fundamentalists like Osama Bin Laden's al-Qua'eda, Hizbullah in Lebanon and the Tamil Tigers of Sri Lanka are not averse to pocketing substantial amounts of money from the cannabis trail in their country.

THE RIF FIGHTS BACK

The so far unchecked rise in cannabis production and distribution in the former communist states does not mean that the traditional heartlands have ceased to be of importance. Far from it. In North Africa, a part of the world that became so dear to the hearts of the thousands of young westerners who stopped there *en route* to India on the Hippie Trail in the late 1960s (see pp17-18), cannabis remains a vital part of the economy. Indeed the vast kif plantations in the Rif Mountains of northwest Morocco are so fruitful that marijuana pollen can often be detected as far away as southern Spain.

The foothills of the mountains are carpeted with plantations, and the illegal money from its cultivation is the primary source of income for the otherwise impoverished peasants who inhabit the local villages. There are thought to be 70,000ha (173,000 acres) of cannabis plantations in the Rif region, which generates around £1 million ($1.5 million). When Morocco gained independence, the government initially planned to ban cannabis growing. But it soon realised this would be impossible; many of the leading figures in the struggle for independence were drug smugglers, regarded as heroes among the local people. Instead, King Mohamed V granted the inhabitants of the Rif the 'privilege' of being allowed to grow cannabis legally.

But while growing it is legal, it is forbidden to transport or sell it. Money talks, however, and police and officials are easily bribed as the product makes its way to Tangiers, Melilla and Ceuta on the North African coast, for shipment to southern Europe.

In this fertile land, cannabis is king. Plantations cover steep manmade terraces that have been razed of trees so that the sun-loving plant is not obscured by foliage. Whole communities dedicate their lives to the plant; women do the hard work such as watering and weeding, while the men do the processing. Ironically, few locals smoke kif. Their view is that, as Muslims, it is okay to cultivate the plant but its consumption should be left to 'the Arabs'.

Once the female plants (male plants do not contain the narcotic), have reached maturity, their flowering tips are cut off. The yield per hectare (2½ acres) is around 400-500kg (880-1,100lb). As a kilogram (2¼lb) of cannabis at this point is worth just less than £6 ($8.70), farmers earn about £3,000 ($4,300) per hectare (2½ acres) - this is at least ten times what they would get for a crop of barley or wheat.

Rif farmers make even more profit by processing the plant on the site. First, the leaves are turned into fine powder by a process of repeated sieving. Experienced workers can turn 100kg (220lb) of cannabis into 4g (⅐oz) of powder; the powder sells for up to £400 ($580) per kilogram (2¼lb) to the traffickers who then refine it into resin for transportation abroad. The relationship between the grower and the trafficker is very much hand-in-glove: drug cartels are happy to allow others to deal with the painstaking cultivation of the cannabis plant itself. Similarly, the process by which cannabis is turned into resin is laborious for the farmer but even more lucrative, provided that they have the patience and the materials to do so. A kilo (2¼lb) of resin can sell for up to £900 ($1,300).

> If the cannabis consumed illegally now was produced and taxed in Britain in exactly the same manner as tobacco, some £16 billion ($23.2 billion) in excise taxes could be raised for the Exchequer. That's enough to pay for 5p (7 cents) off the basic rate of income tax.

Such scenes are played out across the world, as otherwise poor peasants turn to lucrative cannabis instead of traditional crops. Floresta, in the northeast state of Pernambuco is dubbed Brazil's marijuana capital. Here, cannabis grows in an area of 26,000sq km (9,880sq miles), which claims to be the biggest growing area in the world. Up until the 1970s peasants planted cotton, but when bicudo pest destroyed crops they decided that a more profitable crop could be their salvation. Cannabis is 200 times more profitable than beans, rice and maize. It is also illegal – but while the Brazilian authorities occasionally launch raids and tear up plants, the growers just move elsewhere.

THE SMUGGLERS

One morning in 1992 a woman walking her dog near Sea Palling, between Great Yarmouth and Cromer in Norfolk, England, came across ten kitbags containing plastic containers of what was apparently sauerkraut. She alerted the police, who opened the containers and discovered 140kg (300lb) of Lebanese Gold cannabis. 'We believe the drugs had been landed by boat and left for collection,' said Assistant Chief Constable Colin Sheppard. 'We would ask other dog walkers to keep their eyes open for strange pieces of flotsam.'

This incident was typical of the drug-smuggling business from the continent into Britain. While cannabis can be moved between the borders of landlocked European countries with relative ease Britain, because it is an island, presents something of a problem to the smuggler. Ports and airports are scrupulously manned by customs officials, making the illegal import of drugs highly risky. Consequently, traffickers are obliged to be increasingly ingenious in their efforts to get their haul ashore, resulting in surreptitious midnight boat drops reminiscent of something from Treasure Island. Norfolk, with its 160km (100 miles) of largely exposed coastline, is a favoured drug-running route. Every year, Norfolk police arrest over 1,000 people on drugs charges. In even more remote Scotland, one of the biggest hauls ever found occurred in the 1970s when several tonnes/tons of cannabis were found washed up on the Mull of Kintyre.

The advent of the Channel Tunnel has provided another popular route. Between 1996 and 1997, seizures of cannabis from vehicles passing under the sea from France leapt threefold to 1,400kg (3,000lb), while the total haul of drugs seized – including cocaine and heroin – had a street value that had doubled up to £17 million ($25 million). Drugs were found in caravans, in the front seat passenger's emergency airbag and even in a false plaster cast on one woman's arm. 600kg (1,300lb) of cannabis resin were found in a fuel tanker's false compartment while at Felixstowe 500kg (1,100lb) of resin were discovered in sealed tins of vegetables. Among the advantages of the undersea network to the smuggler is the fact that it hides the origin of the courier, as everyone goes through France.

Numbers of smugglers on the Eurostar rail link are also increasing, as they realise how easy it is to lose their identity. Traffickers from South American countries can disguise where they have come from by travelling through several countries. A typical route, according to Customs officials at Waterloo International, London (a station that deals with Eurostar passengers), is from Brazil to Portugal, Spain, France and then the UK.

According to customs officials, cross-Channel day trippers are increasingly being used as a cover for international drug traffickers smuggling cannabis into Britain. Couriers posing as day trippers on ferries collect consignments in France, Belgium and Holland and attempt to re-enter the UK through customs, hoping to slip unnoticed among millions of legitimate travellers. Pensioners and young mothers with children are lured into smuggling by big cash payments. In one such incident, a minibus carrying a party of OAPs on a day trip was used to smuggle 156kg (344lb) of cannabis from Belgium. The large numbers of British people who enjoy a day trip to shop at French supermarkets make it increasingly difficult for customs officers, who have found cannabis and other drugs concealed among cases of beer, bags of wine, cheese and salami.

In recent months, US officials have been surprised by the ingenuity of South American, Mexican and European drug-smuggling rings, whose operations virtually shut down in the days after the 11 September terrorist attacks because of dramatically increased security at US borders. At key crossings in California and South Texas, seizures of cannabis doubled from the same period the previous year. From 1 October to 31 December, customs agents seized 19,176kg (42,283lb) of marijuana, worth about $17 million (£11.7 million) to the distributors who sell to the street dealers.

Wearing artificial marijuana headdresses, two girls share a joint at the Smoke-In at Lafayette Park, Washington, DC, on 4 July 2000, demonstrating in favour of the legalization of cannabis.

A rather ostentatious method of smoking, bongs (also known as water pipes) are designed to pass the smoke through water in order to cool and filter it. Cannabis is put in a bowl at one end of a tube and lit, while the other end is in a sealed container partially filled with water. Smoke exits the pipe and bubbles through a layer of water. The smoke is cooled and carcinogens are removed without affecting the active ingredients.

Coffee shops in Amsterdam sell cannabis at around £6 ($8.70) per gram either behind the bar or at a separate window. Many shops have a written menu and display all of the varieties that can be bought in 1g or 2½g bags, or by the gram up to the new 5g (⅙oz) limit. Most outlets provide free rolling papers and little strips of cardboard for roaches, while a few provide pipes and bongs. 'Coffee shops' are not simply euphemistically named – it is considered extremely bad form not to buy something to eat or drink while you smoke.

Arrests in the past few months indicate that smugglers are using creative new tricks, such as traffickers in the Caribbean Sea and the Pacific Ocean who chain drug-filled metal containers to the undersides of luxury cruise ships and send divers to retrieve the booty after the ships dock in US ports. Others use drug-carrying speedboats to cross deep ocean routes in the Caribbean, where Coast Guard cutters have abandoned some anti-drug patrols since 11 September. 'Our adversary is greed and the human imagination,' said Joseph Webber, special agent in charge of the US Customs investigations office for the New York City area.

The latest international review of cannabis by the World Health Organization highlights dangers such as throat and lung cancer and 'increasing incidence of mental health problems due to prolonged heavy use in a minority of users'.

One of Britain's leading drugs traffickers was Curtis 'Cocky' Warren, who grew up in Liverpool's Toxteth estate and rose from abject poverty to be ranked in the top 500 of *The Sunday Times'* 'Rich List', with a fortune estimated conservatively at around £40 million ($58 million) and privately at over £180 million ($260 million). Warren's money was purely a result of the drugs trade. When police raided his Dutch hideout in 1996, they found – along with vast quantities of heroin, ecstasy and cocaine – over 1,500kg (3,300lb) of cannabis resin with a street value of millions.

Warren is now serving 12 years in a Dutch jail and, while customs officers regard this as a success, they also know that his place will already have been filled by opportunist traffickers eager to earn a highly lucrative living importing drugs into Britain from the continent. The number of drug traffickers currently operating the cannabis trail can only be a matter for speculation. Suffice to say, the number still operating far outweighs the number behind bars. For every high-profile syndicate bust, dozens more continue to operate their global business. Indeed the power struggle for the distribution of cannabis and other drugs often only comes to light when it erupts into brutal violence.

An indication of the way the cannabis trail has shifted to eastern Europe is the recent spate of gangland murders involving crime bosses from the former communist states. In December 1999, Andrzej K, a leading drug trafficker from Warsaw, Poland was enjoying a skiing holiday in the winter resort of Zakopane when two men pulled up beside him in a saloon car and shot him twice in the head. Andrzej's murder was just the latest in a spate of drug-related killings across eastern Europe as a vicious turf war over the distribution rights to the CIS's burgeoning cannabis supply spilled into bloodshed. A week earlier, a rival gang member was killed in a car bomb attack in the Slovak capital Bratislava, while in the Croatian capital Zagreb a passerby was killed by a rocket-propelled grenade that bounced off the car it had been fired at.

Even in the UK, the battle for control of the drugs trade can result in gruesome murder. In 1995 three gangsters from Essex – Pat Tate, Tony Tucker and Craig Rolfe – were blasted to death with a shotgun as they sat in a Range Rover in a secluded lane in Rettendon, waiting to conclude a drugs deal. Two members of a rival gang, one of whom had served nine years for importing cannabis, were later sentence to triple life sentences each for the brutal slayings.

In many ways, it is astonishing that the same fate never befell the man widely regarded as being the number one cannabis trafficker in the 1970s and 1980s. Oxford educated Howard Marks built up a worldwide smuggling network that was allegedly responsible for supplying the majority of marijuana smoked in the western world in that period. By the mid-1980s, he owned 25 companies and possessed 43 aliases – among them Mr Nice, which was also the title of his bestselling autobiography. Accused of importing 15 tonnes/tons of cannabis into Scotland in 1981, Marks persuaded the jury that he was in actuality an agent for MI6 and that his drug-smuggling activities were nothing but a front to disguise his attempts to infiltrate the IRA. His acquittal left British Customs and Excise, in the words of one of its senior officials, 'astonished, disbelieving and incredulous'.

Canada became the first country in the world to legalize the use of cannabis for medical purposes in July 2001, allowing those with chronic and terminal illnesses to grow their own and to smoke, inhale in some other way or eat the drug as they preferred.

Earlier, in 1973, Marks had been charged with conspiring to import hashish into the USA, hidden in the speaker systems of non-existent

British rock bands. Allowed out on bail, he disappeared for seven years and, while on the run, actively encouraged the rumour that he had been abducted by the American Mafia. When he was finally caught in 1990, he admitted two counts of racketeering in a federal court in Florida and was sentenced to 25 years. He served seven, and now works for magazines and newspapers as well as touring Britain with his one-man show. In May 2000, he even stood for election for London Mayor representing the Legalize Cannabis Campaign.

'I'm an outlaw, in the true sense of word,' Marks said in an interview in 1998. 'I'm not a petty criminal, I'm someone who refuses to accept that this [cannabis prohibition] law is unworkable. But you can be a gentleman criminal no matter what the crime, and that wasn't me. I was a purist, I smuggled only dope. I would have never smuggled guns. Or cigarettes. Why? Because they're bad for you.'

Marks is estimated to have made more than £48 million ($70 million) from his trafficking activities.

THE DEALERS
Like all profitable businesses, cannabis relies heavily on strong distribution chains to get it from the supplier into the hands of the customer. And, like warring supermarkets, suppliers will try any innovation in order to give them an edge over their rivals. The advent of the Internet, in particular, has been exploited by dealers who have been able to expand from back-street transactions to global deals and virtual home delivery at the click of a mouse. However, the illegality of cannabis means that those distribution chains are largely shrouded in secrecy. The casual user will purchase his or her supply from a dealer in a pub or during a house call, but from there the trail gets less easy to follow.

What is clear is that cannabis suppliers on the continent rely upon a network of middlemen and sales operatives to distribute the drugs on the ground. The network has to be secure, which means that various levels of operatives are often kept in the dark.

As one London-based dealer explained: 'As far as I am concerned, I get the dope from somebody higher up the chain. I don't know who he is, or who he works for. To be honest, my view is the less I know about it, the better. I'd guess there are probably another two or three above him before you get to the main man, and I bet nobody knows who that is unless they are his best mates. I know there are gangs in London involved, but I reckon most of them are just in the distribution business. They'll all be getting their shit from someone higher up the chain.

The usual format is that we meet at a pre-ordained location, usually his flat, and he will hand over the resin or the weed. The amount depends, as does the price, on the quality of the shit. I'll usually buy around a grand's worth off him. It's like going to the wholesalers, I suppose. Then, basically, it's up to me. I've got a fairly steady client base, quite reliable, and I reckon on making a three or four hundred quid [about $500] profit on that initial outlay. There are dealers who rip people off, giving them crap and charging over the odds. But my view is that people are only naïve once, and after that they won't touch you with a bargepole. It just isn't good business. The only people who make a fortune out of this are the traffickers and smugglers. I'm just a minion, the lowest of the low – but that's all right with me. I make enough to get by.'

In the US, the Mafia frowned upon drug dealing for many years. But since the 1970s, the earning potential has proved hard to resist. Hard drugs tend to be the currency used more often than not, but the ready supply of South American marijuana is equally a cash cow for the bosses. Dealing on the streets is rife, and the supply plentiful.

'You think that it's just poor black folks who smoke shit,' said one Harlem dealer. 'You'd be wrong. I've had rich white guys in flash cars pulling up to score on the way home, and high school kids you wouldn't never normally see in this area. In fact, you ever see a white face in Harlem, most times they are looking to score some shit for their weekend parties.'

In Holland, the acceptable face of dealing is in cannabis cafés – but the government restrictions on the amount it is permissible to buy has seen an upsurge in backstreet dealers. In Italy, meanwhile, the government has been keen to remove dealers from the streets with the same broom as they are currently removing lay-by prostitutes – not out of any great legal clampdown, but because they believe such people give the country a bad name among visitors.

Such is the wild west nature of the eastern European drugs trade since the end of communism, the selling of dope is strictly controlled by rival gangs. 'I made a big mistake trying to buy some hash in Moscow when I was there on a visit,' says student Ricky Hunt. 'I found one guy who looked promising – I even saw him dealing to some other people. But when he clocked I was American he ran for the hills. Turns out you got to work for a specific gang to sell to American tourists, because American tourists pay more money. This guy was just selling to the locals. He was small time.'

HOME-GROWN HASH

Not surprisingly, growing your own cannabis is increasing in popularity, given the relative ease with which a crop can be grown. The favoured method is via a hydroponic growing system, in which plants are grown without soil but are fed on nutrients dissolved in a piped water supply and given artificial sunlight with powerful lighting rigs. The technique is much favoured by cannabis growers as it requires very little maintenance. Most systems can be fixed up to timers, avoiding suspicious numbers of journeys to the location. The chemistry behind a hydroponic systems is complex, but getting your hands on one is anything but. A starter kit is available on the Internet for less than £400 ($580). A top-of-the-range kit can cost up to £2,000 ($2,900).

Plant seizures in the UK were up from 11,839 in 1992 to 116,119 in 1996, and these ranged from small garden plots to large, almost industrial-sized factories. One seizure in Exeter discovered hydroponic equipment worth £6,000 ($8,700) and cannabis with a street value of almost £70,000 ($100,000). It's a similar story across Europe: in Germany, a group of neighbours from Munich were discovered to be growing communal hydroponic hash worth in excess of £200,000 ($290,000), while in 1999 alone similar busts in France, Belgium and The Netherlands have netted home-grown cannabis worth over £2 million ($2.9 million). In the United States, the DEA will occasionally make an example of someone caught growing their own, but privately admit it is an impossible task keeping tabs on the estimated nine million hydroponic farmers.

Richard Tamlyn, of the Exeter Drugs Project, is well aware of the huge profits cannabis growers can now make. He says: 'Some of these operations are on a large scale. Run on the lines of a business they involve significant setting up costs, but can bring a considerable return. With all the elements of water, light and heat under artificial control, the plants can be grown for up to 18 hours a day. And, learning from continental cannabis farms, growers will choose to produce the most potent varieties, which in turn fetch the highest prices. It's a long way from the classic image of one man with a couple of plants sat beneath a lightbulb in his bedroom.'

Of course, only a tiny percentage of home-grown hash is destined to be sold on the wider market. The majority is for the personal use of the grower and their friends, thus cutting out the middleman. Indeed such is the popularity of home-grown hash, that research in 2002 suggests that half of the cannabis smoked in Britain is being grown at people's homes rather than being imported by drugs barons, a figure consistent with the rest of Europe. The average cannabis smoker also uses almost twice as much of the drug – 44.5g (1½oz) a year – than they did in 1994, when the figure was 24.8g (⅞oz).

This has led critics to reason that the relaxation of the laws on cannabis possession proposed by some European governments will lead to a steep rise in the number of smokers growing their own supplies without fear of arrest, and believe that a message is being sent out that the drug is safe. However, one leading UK government adviser on drugs believes that cannabis users should be allowed to grow dope plants in their own homes without any fear of being prosecuted. Roger Howard, a member of the Home Office Advisory Group on Drugs said that as David Blunkett, the Home Secretary, has announced that cannabis possession is to be downgraded from a Class B to a Class C offence, it made sense to allow people to grow it. He said: 'As the Government moves towards making small-scale cannabis possession a non-arrestable offence, I hope it will resolve this contradiction by differentiating in law between small-scale cultivation for personal use and large-scale production controlled by organized crime.'

MARIJUANA MONEYSPINNER – WHAT IF IT WERE LEGAL?

Cannabusiness is big business – and one person following the legalization debate with interest is the taxman. Hardly surprising, when figures in the billions are routinely quoted as the income from the illegal cannabis market. Governments, who already cream off substantial amounts in excise duty from drink and tobacco, are all too aware that if the cannabis consumed illegally was produced and taxed exactly like booze and cigarettes, it would raise vast amounts. It's estimated that the US government could swell its coffers by upwards of $400 billion (£276 billion) were it to nationalize its cannabis industry, while most European countries would be looking at an annual windfall of around £16 billion ($23.2 billion). As we have seen, the Dutch taxman already makes a healthy income from cannabis café licences – the amount he could potentially realize if the entire market were taxed would be astronomical.

But how would it work in practice? Where would you buy your legal, government-approved cannabis, and in what form? According to veteran campaigner Steve Abrams, who organized and composed the famous 1967 full-page advertisement in *The Times* demanding decriminalization of the drug, a nationalized cannabis industry, with profits going to the British National Health Service, would boost NHS funds by £2 billion ($2.9 billion) a year 'on conservative estimates'. Abrams believes good-quality cannabis could be grown in sufficient quantity to satisfy domestic demand without the need for imports that would breach Britain's obligations under international treaties. Users would register with their GPs and obtain supplies from chemists.

But if that sounds like too much hassle, don't worry: the tobacco industry have had the whole thing mapped out for years. As early as 1993, anticipating the eventual legalization of the drug, US tobacco giant Philip Morris filed a trademark application for a brand of cannabis cigarette called 'Marley'. Other firms registered names like Acapulco Gold and Red Leb. In 1998, it was revealed that British-American Tobacco had laid down secret plans for cigarettes laced with 'subliminal' levels of marijuana in case the drug was ever legalized.

It may soon be possible to pop down the off-licence and purchase a pack of 20 Acapulco Gold cannabis-laced cigarettes for the price of a normal pack, with between £2 ($2.90) and £3 ($4.35) going to the Treasury in tax. Now that's something for the taxman to put in his pipe and smoke.

ADVERTISING DOPE

America has some of the most stringent laws and restrictions regarding advertising in the world, especially when it comes to billboards on buses and in subway stations. But this did not stop one pro-cannabis campaign group from successfully getting their message across in the capital city.

The ad campaign, which called for the decriminalization of cannabis, was funded by Change the Climate Inc, a non-profit organization that believes the punishment for marijuana use is too harsh. Having already had their campaign rejected by Boston's subway system, they decided to ask officials at Washington's Metro network if they could run their ads during the inauguration month of George W Bush.

'We want the politicians and thousands of people who are going to be here for inauguration month to take an interest in the issue,' said activist Joseph White. 'We like transit agencies because we want to reach average Americans.'

Initially, Metro officials refused the ads, citing a policy that says public service advertising must be non-commercial, non-partisan and 'not designed to influence legislation or public opinion on a controversial subject'. But when threatened with a lawsuit backed by the American Civil Liberties Union arguing that Metro was violating free speech, officials relented.

Change the Climate Inc paid Metro a discounted advertising rate of $2,150 (£1,480) in exchange for illuminated signs on 10 subway platforms, large exterior signs for 50 buses and smaller signs for the interiors of an additional 500 buses. The month-long campaign consisted of three ads. The first, which was put in the stations (including the one closest to the White House) featured a young woman asking, 'Why do kids go to jail for doing what politicians did when they were young? Tell us the truth.'

The second ad, inside buses, showed a business executive with cancer who admitted to smoking marijuana after chemotherapy. The third, which appeared outside the buses, featured two police officers in front of an American flag. It read: 'Police are too important...too valuable...too good...to waste on arresting people for marijuana when real criminals are on the loose.'

White said: 'Most responsible parents don't want their kids smoking marijuana, but we don't want our children arrested, jailed and terrorized in the manufactured hysteria surrounding marijuana.'

Change the Climate Inc plans to expand its transit ads to New York and Chicago. 'We think that having an ad campaign in the nation's capital will make it easier for us in other cities,' White said.

The policy of almost all governments is that cannabis advertising of any sort is prohibited. The Internet, however, has provided a regulation-free billboard for anyone wanting to sell, buy or promote cannabis to a worldwide audience. A world of online cannabis commercials are available 24 hours a day on hundreds of cannabis-related sites available at the click of a mouse. Indeed, traditional methods of advertising have been left behind, leaving governments and drug agencies chasing their tails. And, ironically, for all the millions spent on anti-drug campaigns aimed at highlighting the dangers of narcotics, in some quarters this has proved far more successful for the pro-cannabis lobby than for the government. A survey in the US actually charted an increase in drug use among some teenagers who saw the government's multi-million dollar anti-drug warnings on television.

> 'If I buy a £10 ($15) crack deal, I will be coming back in 10 minutes. If I buy £10 ($15) of cannabis it might last me three or four days. And I don't know anyone who has got addicted to cannabis. A heroin or crack addict has to come back, to get his fix.' Street vendor in Brixton, London

HEMP – THE CANNABIS CASH CROP

Back in the 16th century, marijuana was known as hemp and that substance, in a world where sea power was all important, was crucial in the production of sails. So, as stated before, in 1533 a royal decree was issued in England, forcing farmers to sow part of their land with hemp. The penalty for disobedience was three shillings and fourpence. Thirty years later, under Elizabeth I, the fine had rocketed to £5 (£7.25), underlining the importance naval Britain placed on the cultivation of the tough, fibrous cannabis plant.

The versatility of hemp was not lost on the American pioneers either. Both George Washington and Thomas Jefferson urged colonists to grow the plant, and took the lead by growing it themselves. The fathers of the American nation would therefore have some sympathy with US farming folk today, who are currently fighting a lengthy battle to be allowed to grow hemp on their land *without* being punitively fined.

In May 2000, Maryland became the fourth US state to authorize the production of hemp. To struggling farmers, the decision was a godsend since the bottom had fallen out of the market for tobacco, which was their traditional crop. But the battle had been a long one – because hemp is marijuana, and under federal law, growing marijuana is still illegal.

In the face of sagging farm economies, even the hard-line DEA has reviewed its stance against hemp production. But their involvement in the Maryland project reveals the innate suspicion they still have about marijuana being grown on US soil. Interested farmers face an extensive criminal background check and must be licensed by the DEA. State police are also authorized to search the site at any time. And the law requires agriculture officials to closely control the supply of hemp seeds, which are classified as a controlled substance. The seeds are imported from Canada or further abroad with DEA approval. If, at the end of the four-year pilot scheme, the federal authorities are not convinced, Maryland's farmers will have to dig up their crop and go back to tobacco.

Other than Maryland, only Hawaii, North Dakota and Minnesota have laws allowing hemp production. All were passed in 1999. In Virginia, lawmakers passed a resolution in 2001 urging federal officials to 'revise the necessary regulations' to permit experimental hemp production there. Hawaii, where the DEA claimed most success in its efforts to kick out illegal marijuana cultivation, is ironically the only state so far to receive DEA approval to plant hemp. The site is guarded by a 24-hour alarm system and a 2m- (6½ft) high fence topped with razor wire.

As a mark of solidarity, in the summer of 2001, pro-cannabis campaigner

Grayson Sigler and his wife, Kellie, along with their companions Scott Fur and Charles Ruchalski, spent three months travelling across the US in a hemp-powered Mercedes station wagon, hoping to promote the use of hemp oil as alternative fuel. They used hemp 'biodiesel', which is a thin, oily, bright green liquid made from hemp seed oil through a process called trans-esterification.

'Not being used to hashish...he burst into extraordinary hilarity and filled the hall with shouts of laughter. A moment later he collapsed backwards onto the marble floor and fell prey to hallucinations.'

- From *The Arabian Nights*, 'The Tale Of The Hashish Eater', c1100

'And so you think that opium smoking as seen in the foul cellars of Mott Street and elsewhere is the only form of narcotic indulgence of any consequence in this city, and that hashish, if used at all, is only smoked by a few scattered individuals? Well you are far from right... There is a large community of hashish smokers in this city who are daily forced to indulge their morbid appetites, and I can take you to a house uptown where hemp is used in every conceivable form...'

- From *A Hashish House In New York*, HH Kane, 1870

'Fragrant smoke from the Arabian plant's brown juices creates a swirling dance of powerful fantasies...'

- Maurice von Schwind, 1875.

Cannabis has been described as 'the world's most extraordinary plant' and there can be little argument with that claim. Even without the obvious psychotropic effects of smoking cannabis, this surprisingly flimsy, fork-leafed plant has had a fundamental impact on human civilization from its very earliest days centuries ago because of its sheer versatility – it can be used as a source of building materials and food and medicine.

But of course, it is as a drug that cannabis has found fame and infamy for most of recorded history. When we think of it in terms of pot, hash or any of the multifarious terms dreamed up to describe the plant in its narcotic state, we think of spaced-out hippies protesting against the Vietnam War, dancing like shamen to Jefferson Airplane at Woodstock or marching defiantly behind banners demanding its immediate legalization. We think of Amsterdam cafés filled with pungent fug, laid-back Haight-Ashbury in 1967 and the chaos and culture of Marrakesh in 1970. We think of dope icons like Bob Marley, Bob Dylan, the Beatles and the Fabulous Furry Freak Brothers. In short, we think of a youthful generation finding its voice against the smothering social and legal constraints of the 'square' establishment.

But it must be remembered that all this is merely a snapshot of the last 40 years. In cannabis terms, that is a blink of an eye. Indeed, it demeans the impact of cannabis to think only in terms of its recent history. Even when the Greek historian Herodotus first stumbled upon what must have been to his eyes mind-blowing Scythian cannabis rituals in 450 BC, the plant had been regarded as sacred for over 2,000 years. While it's understandable that Herodotus should wish to record the graphic details of the stoned Scythians for his audience back home, it is a shame that he did so because this is the one aspect that has influenced our perception of cannabis ever since. The paranoid fear about the effects of cannabis on people's minds, personified by Harry J Anslinger in the USA in the 1930s, not to mention the worldwide ban on growing the plant, would have been unfathomable to the ancient Chinese, Indians and Persians. To them, the current wrangling about whether to legalize the drug for medical use would have been laughable. Cannabis *was* a drug for medical use. Its hallucinogenic side effects were pleasant, but they were by no means the be-all and end-all.

The last 2,000 years of the cannabis story have been a lot more fraught than the first 2,000. In AD 70, Dioscorides talked of the widespread use of cannabis as a medicine in Rome, but that is one of the last times it was referred to in purely medicinal terms – up until the 16th century that is. The writing was on the wall 130 years later when Galen described dinner parties in the same city being enlivened by the consumption of weed. But, by then, medical science had progressed; cannabis was just one substance in a growing global pharmacopoeia and people were beginning to use it more as a social drug. The anti-cannabis edicts of the next 1,000 years reflected the fear among spiritual leaders like Ottoman Emir Soudoun Scheikhouni and Pope Innocent VIII that the drug is ruinous to society – and more particularly to their control over it. This is a common refrain that can be found right up to the present day.

The roots of western society's paranoia about cannabis are to be found in its equal paranoia about the east. Wars and geography had kept weird and ungodly eastern culture at arm's length for centuries – but when cannabis, the drug of the heathen, began sweeping across Europe and into the USA there was nothing anyone could do to stop it. And what made matters worse for God-fearing folk was the enthusiasm with which the drug was taken up by their own people. To them, to read excitable reports of bohemians experimenting with hash in New York, London and Paris must have seemed like the end of the world was nigh.

In the 20th century, nowhere was this better illustrated than in the USA. To waspish North Americans, cannabis equated to everything bad that threatened their largely delusionary existence: namely blacks, Mexicans and jazz music. They claimed to fear for the health and well-being of their children, but in reality they were panicking about themselves and their future as the dominant race on the continent. It was the Americans who petitioned the world for a ban on cannabis – not out of some sort of global philanthropism, but because they wanted to stop it flooding into their own country. The fear spread like wildfire; the British couldn't give two hoots about cannabis in 1901, and the Royal Commission concluded that it wasn't harmful enough to bother prohibiting. Within 30 years, however, they had followed the lead of the Geneva Conference on Opium and issued a draconian set of laws banning this 'dangerous drug'.

Again we must turn to the role played by Harry J Anslinger in all this, for he is the pivotal figure in the modern cannabis story. It has been suggested that Anslinger was just a regular guy doing his job. But what *was* Anslinger's job? As an arch-propagandist of the evils of cannabis, there is no doubt that he was without equal. His *Reefer Madness* diatribe was a masterpiece of hyperbole, paranoia and racist rabble-rousing. But at the end of the day Anslinger failed abjectly in his true aim, which was to rid the spectre of cannabis from American society. Indeed, it's arguable that Anslinger switched more all-American kids onto cannabis out of sheer curiosity than he prevented from trying it. The young people at the heart of the 1960s drug-taking scene in America were the same generation Anslinger had been trying to save from 'reefer madness'.

The 1960s are held up as cannabis's golden era but, to all but a few die-hard pot-heads, a joint was little more than a symbol of the turbulent times. People changed the world, not cannabis, despite what some may think, and today the kaftaned tokers preaching love and peace in San Francisco and Woodstock look horribly dated and more than a little ludicrous. Many of them, now middle aged and respectable, look back on those days with embarrassment. Similarly, choreographed legalization marches and full page ads in *The Times* signed by celebrities may have seemed like big news at the time, but their effect was negligible; if anything the 1970s and 1980s marked a period of sustained governmental oppression on drug taking that Harry J Anslinger could only have dreamed about. The 1960s were 'Cannabis – the cabaret years'. There was glamour, tinsel and lots of noise, but there was little substance.

Since then, Holland has been held up as a model for modern cannabis use. The laid-back cafés of Amsterdam are the perfect example of how soft drug taking, properly regulated, can have a place in modern society. Again, the jury is out on this one. Holland's relaxed laws have made it not only a Mecca for cannabis enthusiasts, but a centre for global drug trafficking. In a world where drugs are banned, a country that lowers its guard is one that is ripe for exploitation. It is all very well sitting in a café enjoying a civilized spliff, but if traffickers from Azerbaijan are scoring deals in the adjacent alleyway then it rather sours the experience.

Experts have yet to make a definitive link between cannabis and the numbers of heroin junkies littering Dam Square – but it would stand to reason that even if cannabis is not a 'gateway' drug to the hard stuff, the very culture of the country is conducive to substance abuse of one sort or another. Until the rest of the world follows Holland's lead – which simply will not happen in the foreseeable future – then cannabis cafés are more dangerous than they are worth.

It is only since the mid-1990s that we have entered a rational debate about cannabis. Ironically, the catalyst for the current move towards decriminalization has not been protest but a renewed appreciation of the drug's medicinal qualities – the same qualities that first attracted ancient man to the plant in the first place. Progress has, as ever, been painfully slow. In the UK, successive Home Secretaries have been too scared of the political fall out to sanction any definite action. Even Jack Straw, who at one stage filled the pro-cannabis lobby with hope, bailed out hopelessly at the crucial moment. It has taken a Home Secretary with the courage of David Blunkett to actually make the first move. He has, of course, been cunning: there are still years of clinical trials to be completed before legislation is rubber-stamped, and by then David Blunkett will be long gone. But he has done enough. When even Cabinet ministers feel confident enough to admit that – shock horror! – they smoked dope like the rest of the population, the momentum, one feels, is nigh-on unstoppable.

It is a movement that is gathering pace across the more enlightened EU countries and one that will result in a decriminalization of cannabis for medicinal use sooner rather than later. Whether this will lead to full legalization is another matter, and for most politicians this is as yet a step too far. The most likely scenario is that strictly regulated personal use of cannabis will eventually be sanctioned, with the respective governments raking in revenue from licensed outlets and the products themselves being made by multi-national tobacco companies. But if it happens, it must happen across the board: there is no point in German off-licences selling 20 Aruba Golds if Austria's don't. The only people who benefit from a scenario like this are the drug traffickers.

Even then, it is likely that the USA will be left out in the cold. Bill Clinton's laughable admission that he smoked but didn't inhale says much about the American establishment's on-going cannabis guilt. When a supposedly liberal-minded US president would rather admit to screwing an intern in the Oval Office than to smoking a joint, it seems inconceivable that any future administration would even dream of relaxing the laws on cannabis. The election of ultra-conservative Republican George W Bush to the White House would appear to be the final nail in the coffin – for the time being, at least.

Whatever the outcome, one thing is for certain: the 'world's most extraordinary plant' will continue to weave its extraordinary influence on us for as long as it finds soil to grow in. Four thousand years is a long time to walk hand-in-hand with something we still can't fully understand – but it is, I suspect, only the beginning of the story.

GLOSSARY

Anslinger, Harry J - legendary US anti-drugs enforcer, author of *Reefer Madness*

Bale - compressed block of marijuana, usually between 4.5-18kg (10-40lb)

Bhang - an Indian and Middle Eastern smoking mixture consisting of pollen from marijuana flowers and ghee, an oily butter

Bifta - a cone-shaped joint

Blazed - term used to describe a feeling of being totally high

Block-up - a feeling of cannabis intoxication, ie 'I'm totally block-up'

Blunt - a joint rolled in the tobacco-leaf wrapper of a Phillies Blunt cigar

Bogart - to hog the joint

Bong - a water-cooled pipe for one smoker, usually made of bamboo or glass

Brick - a cube of compressed cannabis weighing 1kg (2¼lb)

Bucket - unusual smoking device made from a bucket filled with water, a bottle with its base removed and a pipe in the top

Bud - the fresh or dried flowers of the female marijuana plant

Bhudda stick - another name for *Thai stick*

Cannabis indica - scientific name for a species of marijuana plant, the Indian hemp

Cannabis sativa - strain of cannabis most popularly used for smoking

Cheech and Chong - Cult 1970s *pot-heads* responsible for comedy records and films

Chiba-Chiba - a Brazilian form of pot, usually compressed into *bricks*

Chillum/chalice - a small cone-shaped pipe made of clay, or sometimes fruit and vegetable rinds

Chronic - high-quality or potent joint

Cocktail - a joint of combined tobacco and marijuana

Colombian - the most common type of grass

Doobie - joint. The term originated in the 1960s and 1970s on the cult US TV show *Romper Room*, where the good children were called 'Good Do-Bes'. It was later popularized by *Cheech and Chong* and the *Fabulous Furry Freak Brothers*

Donovan - 1960s UK folk singer who became the first celebrity to be busted for cannabis possession in 1965

Dope - any controlled substance, although usually refers to marijuana or heroin

Durban Brown - Marijuana from the Natal Province of South Africa

Dylan, Bob - US folk singer who advocated marijuana and is thought to have introduced the drug to The Beatles

Elbow - 0.45kg (1lb) of pot

Fabulous Furry Freak Brothers - Cult cartoon characters created by Gilbert Shelton in 1970

Fresh - great, good, grand. 'That's fresh!' Also refers to having a plentiful *stash*

Froggy - refers to a dry mouth after smoking

Gage - 1940s slang for pot

Ganja - Jamaican/Indian term for pot

Gold - yellow pot from Acapulco, Mexico

Grass - cannabis, marijuana, weed

Hash(ish) - smoking mixture that varies by region. It is primarily associated with resin obtained from Middle Eastern or Indian marijuana

Hemp - stalk and stem of the cannabis plant, traditionally used to make rope and fabric

Herb - Jamaican term for marijuana. Derived from biblical references

Hippie Trail - popular route taken by 1960s pot-heads, which went from Morocco to India and incorporated many hash shops

Hogleg - large, overfilled joint that looks like a hog's leg

Hookah - hashish water pipe with four stems that enables four people to smoke at the same time. Used by the caterpillar in *Alice In Wonderland*

Jefferson airplane - 1930s US term used for a *roach* holder fashioned from a matchbook cover. Later the name of a hippie band fronted by Grace Slick

Jive - slang word for the marijuana-influenced music and dancing of 1930s and 1940s America

Johnson - 1960s US term for a joint, as in 'Gimme a toke on that johnson, man'

Joint - marijuana cigarette, also known as a jay

Kief/kif/kaff/khayf - golden pollen hash from Morocco, Lebanon and other Middle East nations

Lambsbread - large *buds* from Jamaica, shaped like a lamb's tail, that can be carved like a loaf of bread

Marijuana - term popularized in Mexico (translation means intoxicated) for the smokable flowers and leaves of the female cannabis plant

Marley, Bob - Jamaican musician who promoted the use of *herb* through Rastafarianism

Maryjane/MJ - female cannabis plant. Male plants have almost no active *tetrahydrocannabinol*

Mezz - another name for marijuana. Derived from Mezz Mezzrow, 1930s jazzman and dope dealer who supplied the New Orleans jazz greats such as Louis Armstrong

Monged - describes the tiredness smokers feel when they come down from a high - 'I'm monged'

Muggles - US term for marijuana, which originated in the 1930s

Munchies - insatiable appetite following marijuana smoking

Nickel bag - US term for $5 (£3.45) worth of marijuana

Oil - purified and concentrated resin from hashish or marijuana

Oz - 1oz (28g) of pot

Paraquat - weedkiller that has been used by the American government to destroy cannabis plantations since the 1970s. It led to the great Paraquat Scare of 1976, where *pot-heads* believed they were smoking contaminated marijuana

Panama Red - potent strain of marijuana from Panama

Pot - cannabis, marijuana, grass

Pot-head - devotee of marijuana

Reefer - turn-of-the-century term for marijuana that is still in popular use today

Rizla - brand of cigarette papers used for rolling joints

Roach - cardboard filter used in joints

Rope dope - low-quality pot from a leafy hemp

Shit - another name for cannabis

Sinsemilla - flowering tops of seedless plants

Skunk - aromatic sinsemilla, usually cultivated from Afghani marijuana

Smoke - another term for pot, marijuana, reefer, grass etc

Soma - British protest group (named after the drug in Aldous Huxley's *Brave New World*) who sent a full-page letter to *The Times* demanding the legalization of cannabis in 1967

Spliff - Jamaican term for a joint, now popular worldwide

Stash - supply of dope, usually hidden

Stoned - intoxicated by marijuana

Tea - Slang for marijuana

Tea pad - Illicit marijuana den popular in 1930s New York

THC/tetrahydrocannabinol - psychoactive cannabinoid in marijuana that is responsible for the high

Thai stick - variety of marijuana usually wrapped around thin bamboo splints

Thyme - spice commonly used by dealers to defraud customers because it looks like marijuana

Toke - to inhale/puff from a joint

Toklas, Alice B - creator of a cult hashish fudge

Twigs and seeds - unsmokable leftovers from screening marijuana before sale, or the detritus in the bottom of the bag after purchase

Viper - name given to people who frequented *tea pads* and smoked *jive* - derives from the hissing noise they made when inhaling smoke

Wasted - term meaning 'out of your brain' on weed

Weed - another term for marijuana, grass, reefer, etc

Zonked - wasted

Zig-zag - popular brand of US rolling papers famous for the silhouette of a bearded smoker on the label

TIMELINE

2700 BC: First recorded use of cannabis as a medicine, in China

1200 BC: Cannabis mentioned in the sacred Hindu text *Atharvaveda* as 'sacred grass', one of the five sacred plants of India. It is used as an offering to Shiva

550 BC: The Persian prophet Zoroaster writes the *Zend-Avesta*, a sacred text that lists more than 10,000 medicinal plants. Hemp is at the top of the list

500 BC: Hemp is introduced into the countries of northern Europe for the first time by the Scythians of Asia

430 BC: Greek historian Herodotus observes the ritual and recreational use of cannabis by the Scythians

AD 70: Dioscorides mentions the widespread use of cannabis as a medicine in Rome

AD 200: Roman historian Galen observes that it is sometimes 'customary to give Hemp to guests to promote hilarity and enjoyment'

AD 800: Islamic prophet Mohammed permits cannabis use – but forbids alcohol

1100: Cannabis smoking is, by now, commonplace in the Middle East

1150: Moslems use cannabis to start Europe's first paper mill, mashing the hemp leaves into pulp and rolling them into tough parchment

1200: Arab traders take cannabis to the Mozambique coast of Africa

1378: One of the first dissenting voices is heard when Ottoman Emir Soudoun Scheikhouni issues an edict against eating cannabis

1430: Joan of Arc is accused of using herbal 'witch drugs' such as cannabis to hear voices

1484: Pope Innocent VIII labels cannabis as an unholy sacrament of the Satanic mass and issues a papal ban on cannabis medicines

1533: The use of hemp for fabric assumes vital importance in naval Britain, where it is used to make sails. Henry VIII issues a decree in 1533 that for every 60 acres (24ha) of arable land a farmer owned, a quarter acre (0.1ha) was to be sown with hemp. The penalty for not doing so was to be three shillings and four pence

1563: Queen Elizabeth I orders landowners with 60 acres (24ha) or more to grow cannabis or face a £5 ($7.25) fine

1564: King Philip of Spain orders cannabis to be grown throughout his empire, from Argentina to Oregon

1597: English physician John Gerard recommends cannabis as it 'consumeth wind and dryeth up seed [semen]'

1650: Cannabis becomes a major trade item between central and southern Asia. Its recreational use spreads across the Middle East and Asia

1653: English physician Nicholas Culpeper claims cannabis 'allayeth inflamations, easeth the pain of gout, tumours or knots of joints, pain of hips'

1798: While in Egypt, Napoleon is stunned by the use of cannabis among the lower classes. He bans it – but his soldiers take the pastime of cannabis smoking back to France with them

1840: Cannabis-based medicines become available in the USA, while cannabis is sold in Persian pharmacies. Le Club Hachichins, or Hashish Eater's Club, is established in Paris

1842: Cannabis becomes a popular medicine in Victorian England, used to treat ailments such as muscle cramps, menstrual cramps, rheumatism and the convulsions of tetanus, rabies and epilepsy

1883: Hashish houses become commonplace in America

1890: Queen Victoria is prescribed cannabis for period pains. Her personal doctor, Sir Robert Russell, claims: 'It is one of the most valuable medicines we possess.' In the same year, it is made illegal in Greece and Turkey

1901: The British Royal Commission concludes that cannabis is relatively harmless and not worth prohibiting

1915-27: Cannabis is prevented for non-medical use in California (1915), Texas (1919), Louisiana (1924) and New York (1927)

1924: Cannabis is outlawed by the Geneva Conference on Opium

1928: The Dangerous Drugs Act makes cannabis illegal in Britain

1937: The US Federal government outlaws cannabis. The Federal Bureau of Narcotics prosecutes 3,000 doctors for 'illegally' prescribing cannabis-derived medicines. Its chief, Harry Anslinger, writes the polemic Marijuana: Assassin Of Youth

1967: Mick Jagger and Keith Richards of the Rolling Stones are sentenced to prison for smoking cannabis. A 'Legalize Pot' rally is held in Hyde Park, London. An advert in The Times, paid for by Beatle Paul McCartney, states: 'The law against marijuana is immoral in principle and unworkable in practice.' Signatories include The Beatles, author Graham Greene, Jonathan Aitken and eccentric psychiatrist RD Laing

1969: The Rolling Stones hold a free concert in Hyde Park, London, during which an organization called the Bong Parade pass a foot-long joint among the crowd

There is mass use of the drug at Woodstock

1971: The UK reinforces its anti-cannabis stand with the Misuse Drugs Act. The plant and its resin are classified as Class B drugs, cannabis oil Class A, while cannabis itself is defined as Schedule 1 – of no therapeutic use

1973: The Drugs Enforcement Administration (DEA) is set up in the United States and vows to destroy all marijuana cultivated on its own soil

1976: The Dutch authorities legalize the sale of cannabis in dedicated cannabis cafés

1980: Paul McCartney is busted for cannabis possession at Tokyo airport and spends ten days in jail

1981: Direct action group Smokey Bear sends cannabis plants to 60 English MPs

1990: Los Angeles Police Chief Darryl Gates testifies before the US Senate Judiciary Committee that 'casual drug users should be taken out and shot'

1992: President Bill Clinton admits to having smoked cannabis – but claims he never inhaled

1996: Clinton employs General Barry McCaffrey as his new, hard-hitting drugs tsar. Transform, the campaign to liberalize drug policy and legislation, is launched. Several US states allow medicinal cannabis to be distributed in special 'cannabis clubs'

1997: William Straw, son of British Home Secretary Jack Straw, is arrested for dealing cannabis, following a *Daily Mirror* sting. He is cautioned by police. The new Labour government appoints Keith Hellawell, former Chief Constable, as the new drugs tsar. *The Independent On Sunday* launches a campaign to decriminalize cannabis. Editor Rosie Boycott keeps a cannabis plant in her office

The Alliance for Cannabis Therapeutics launches a major advertising campaign in the national press for the legalization of marijuana for medical use

1998: *The Independent On Sunday*'s campaign culminates in a march on Trafalgar Square, which attracts thousands of supporters

2000: English Prime Minister Tony Blair agrees that cannabis should be legalized for medical purposes. His Home Secretary Jack Straw refuses to do so

The Police Foundation Report suggests that certain drugs be reclassified and penalties reduced. The government rejects the recommendations

Staunch right wing newspaper the *Daily Mail* calls for a 'mature and rational' debate on the drugs issue. The *Daily Telegraph* suggests an 'experiment with legalization'

General Barry McCaffrey loses his job as US drugs tsar

2001: Canada becomes the first country in the world to legalize cannabis for medical use. Portugal, Belgium and Switzerland all make the first moves towards decriminalizing the drug

David Blunkett, the new British Home Secretary, sacks Keith Hellawell. He gives tacit support to a scheme in Brixton, South London where police will not arrest people using cannabis. He also announces that cannabis is to be reclassified from a Class B drug to a Class C drug, putting it on a par with amphetamines.

SOURCES AND RECOMMENDED READING

Boyd, Neil: *High Society* (Key Porter Books, 1991)

British Medical Association: *Therapeutic Uses Of Cannabis* (Taylor & Francis, 1997)

D'Oudney, JR and D'Oudney, KEA: *Cannabis: The Facts, Human Rights And The Law* (Scorpio, 2000)

Estren, Mark J: *A History Of Underground Comics* (Straight Arrow Books, 1974)

Frank, Mel: *The Marijuana Grower's Guide* (Publishers Group West, 1997)

Gold, D: *Cannabis Alchemy: The Art Of Modern Hashmaking: Methods For Preparation Of Extremely Potent Cannabis Products* (Ronin Publishing, 1990)

Gottlieb, Adam: *Ancient And Modern Methods Of Growing Extraordinary Marijuana* (Ronin Publishing, 1998)

Grossman, Andre: *Greetings From Cannabis Country* (Green Candy Press, 2001)

Grotenherman, Franjo and Russo, Ethan (editors): *Cannabis And Cannabinoids: Pharmacology, Toxicology, And Therapeutic Potential* (Integrative Healing Press, 2001)

Health and Safety Executive: *Pilot Study: Effects Of Cannabis* (HSE, 2000)

Herer, Jack: *The Emperor Wears No Clothes: The Authoritative Historical Record Of The Cannabis Plant, Marijuana Prohibition And How Hemp Can Still Save The World* (Green Planet Co, 1998)

High Times Greatest Hits (Trans-High Corp, 1994)

Iverson, Lesley: *The Science Of Marijuana* (Oxford University Press, 2000)

King, Jason: *The Cannabible* (Ten Speed Press, 2001)

Matthews, Patrick: *Cannabis Culture* (Bloomsbury, 2000)

McAllister, William: *Drug Diplomacy In The 20th Century: An International History* (Routledge, 1999)

Morgan, John P and Zimmer, Lynn: *Marijuana Myths, Marijuana Facts* (Lindesmith Center, 1997)

Nelson, Robert A and Robinson, Rowan: *The Great Book Of Hemp: The Complete Guide To The Commercial, Medicinal And Psychotropic Uses Of The World's Most Extraordinary Plant* (Park Street Press, 1995)

Police Foundation: *Drugs And The Law: Report Of The Independent Inquiry Into The Misuse Of Drugs Act 1971*

Potter, Beverly and Joy, Dan: *The Healing Magic Of Cannabis* (Ronin Publishing, 1998)

Ratsch, Christian: *Marijuana Medicine: A World Tour Of The Healing And Visionary Powers Of Cannabis* (Healing Art Press, 2001)

Select Committee on Science and Technology: *Therapeutic Uses Of Cannabis: Government Response To The Report* (HMSO Books, 2001)

Sherman, Carol and Smith, Andrew: *Highlights: An Illustrated History Of Cannabis* (Ten Speed Press, 1999)

Solman, Larry: *Reefer Madness* (Grove Press, 1979)

Storm, Daniel: *Marijuana Hydroponics* (And/Or Books, 1986)

Therapeutic Uses Of Cannabis With Evidence: House Of Lords Papers (HMSO Books, 2001)

Witton, John: *Cannabis: The Facts* (Avebury Technical, 2002)

INDEX

Also available
in this series